Advertising-
How to write
the kind
that works
REVISED EDITION

Advertising-
How to write the kind that works

REVISED EDITION

DAVID L. MALICKSON
Professor of Advertising
University of Florida

JOHN W. NASON
Vice President, Director of Marketing
Selchow & Righter Company

Charles Scribner's Sons • New York

Copyright © 1977, 1982 David L. Malickson and John W. Nason

Library of Congress Cataloging in Publication Data

Malickson, David L.
  Advertising—how to write the kind that works.

  Includes index.
  1. Advertising copy. 2. Advertising layout and
typography. I. Nason, John W. II. Title.
HF5825.M27 1982   659.1   82–6028
ISBN 0–684–17631–9
ISBN 0–684–17632–7 (pbk.)

Portions of this book previously appeared in *From Hed
to Logo,* copyright © 1973 D. Malickson

1 3 5 7 9 11 13 15 17 19 F/C 20 18 16 14 12 10 8 6 4 2
1 3 5 7 9 11 13 15 17 19 F/P 20 18 16 14 12 10 8 6 4 2

PRINTED IN THE UNITED STATES OF AMERICA

To Philip and Sarah Malickson,
Crickett, Darby, Debby
and over 3,000 students
I have enjoyed teaching.—DLM

To all those who, over the years,
expressed their confidence
in a concrete way:
by entrusting to me
more than a quarter-billion
advertising dollars to spend wisely.—JWN

Contents

About the authors   xiii

Preface   xvii

1 Introduction   1

The Buck Stops with You   2

How to Get Started   3

2 Organization and relationships   5

Advertising Agencies   6
*Creative Development · 8   Finishing the
Job · 10   Agency Compensation · 10   Local
Rates · 11   What the 15% Commission
Buys · 12   How to Pick an Agency · 13*

Retail Advertising   14
Newspaper Ad Departments   15
One-Person Organizations   16
Marketing   17
Merchandising   18
Public Relations   19
Living with Your Artist   21
Living with Your Client   21
Living with Your Friends   22

3 The medium and your message

25

Media Efficiency   26
Looking at Newspapers   28
*Ad Placement · 29   Small Space · 31
Newspaper Color · 33   Classified
Advertising · 33   Weekly Newspapers · 34
Printed Inserts · 34*

Dialing in Radio   35
The TV Picture   36
Magazine Opportunities   37
*Regional Editions · 38   Preferred Positions · 40
Unusual Positions · 41   The Press of
Business · 43*

Sales Displays (Point-of-Purchase)   43
Outdoor Advertising   44
Direct Mail   46
Transit Advertising   48
Advertising Specialties   50
Directories   50
Other Media   51

4 Applying psychology

52

Teach, Don't Tell   53
Choose Your Target   53

Do Your Own Research   56
Common Sense   56
Two Rules to Remember   57
Benefit Selection   58
Help Solve Problems   59
Smiles Mean Sales   60
Unique Selling Proposition   61
*USPs for National Ads · 61   USPs for Retail
Ads · 66   USPs for Trade Ads · 67   USPs for
Industrial Ads · 68   USPs for Professional
Ads · 68   Building a Foundation · 71*

AIDA   75
Two Simple Rules   76
Positive vs. Negative   77

5 Basic writing style

79

Clarity   79
Ten Timely Tips   80
Choppy Copy   82
The Writing Yardstick   83
*A Tool for More Effective Writing · 83   How
to Use the Writing Yardstick · 83*

Copyreading Symbols   85

6 Basic print techniques

88

Anatomy of Print Ads   88
Internal Communication   90
Copy Sheet   92
Doodle   94
Rough Layout   96
Keying   101
Making Your Job Easier   103
Design   103
Eyeflow · 105   Balance · 108   Dominance · 108

Clip Art   110

7 Copywriting for different print media 113

Newspapers 113
Magazines 115
Direct Response 121
Direct Mail 121
*Using Gimmicks · 123   Multiple Mailings · 124
Building Store Traffic · 124   Some
Warnings · 125*

Magazine Mail Order 125
Coupons · 126   Split Runs · 126

Outdoor 128

8 Copywriting for broadcast media 130

Radio 131
*Music · 132   Sound Effects · 133   Format · 133
Recording Radio Spots · 134*

Television 137
*Show and Sell · 138   Hold Your Audience · 141
Script Format · 141   Getting Started · 142
Film or Tape · 143*

9 Campaign planning 147

Competitive Pressure 148
Don't Expect Miracles 149
National Campaigns 150
Company Promotions 151
*Demographic Groups · 151   Service
Campaigns · 152*

Institutional Advertising   153
Retail Campaigns   156
Retail Tactics · 157   Building Image · 158
Long-Range Goals · 159

The Importance of Being Different   160
Slogans   160
Unstated Themes   161
State Your Objectives   162
Campaign Life   164
Flights · 166   Local Follow-Up · 167

Non-campaign Ads   167

10 Merchandising your advertising

169

"Selling" the Sales Force   170
Enlisting Dealer Support   171
Co-op Advertising   173
Media Assistance   177
Retail Ad Merchandising   179
Whose Job?   179

11 Copy research

182

Living with Research   183
Market Studies   184
Designing the Market Survey · 184   Judging
Research Results · 185

Pre-testing Techniques   186
Focus Groups · 187   Individual Reactions · 189
Alternate Executions · 190

Post-testing Ads   190
Post-testing Commercials   191
Test Markets   192
Some Precautions   192

12 Production pitfalls

195

Communication   196
Typesetting   196
Paste-ups   197
Illustrations   198
Printing   199

Postscript

202

Helpful resources

207

Publications   207
Media Associations   208
Research Organizations   210
Miscellaneous   210

Index   213

About the authors

DAVID L. MALICKSON started his advertising career at a major Philadelphia department store. After serving in the U.S. Air Force as an Information Officer, he joined the New Holland Division of Sperry Rand Corporation as an advertising supervisor for farm equipment.

Following his agricultural experience in industrial advertising, Professor Malickson helped launch the mass merchandising of women's high-fashion wigs as the Advertising and Marketing Director for a little-known company in the beauty world whose annual sales zoomed from $100,000 to $5 million in three short years. The firm eventually packaged wigs for Sears, Roebuck and Co., as well as for the Hazel Bishop and Schiaparelli labels and many national private-label corporations. He is known to many as the "father of the mass-merchandised wig" because he applied the ready-to-wear concept to this product. He was also responsible for many other major firms showing an interest in this beauty item. He served as a consultant in the early history of mass-merchandised wigs working for corporations such as the Colgate-

Palmolive Company, the Toni Company, Procter & Gamble, and others.

Professor Malickson graduated from Pennsylvania State University and has an advanced degree in Public Communications from Boston University. He has taught at the Charles Morris Price Professional School in Philadelphia, Drake University, and at the University of Florida in Gainesville since 1969. He also conducts national workshops and seminars for professional and retail organizations.

JOHN W. NASON is a veteran advertising executive who spent over 25 years writing copy at several major advertising agencies. During 18 years of service at J. Walter Thompson Company, longtime leader among the world's advertising agencies, he rose through the creative ranks to the position of associate creative director. Each year he wrote millions of dollars worth of advertising for products and services ranging from hair shampoo to motor oil, from airline services to health insurance. His most recent specialty was corporate advertising, in which a company's good reputation is presented as a reason to prefer its offerings, a factor that is assuming greater importance in an era of parity products.

Recently, Mr. Nason chose to leave the agency field and join forces with one of his clients as Marketing Vice President. Selchow & Righter company is a major game manufacturer; its best known product is Scrabble® Brand Crossword Game. He is responsible for organizing the full panoply of marketing services while overseeing a multimillion dollar advertising and public relations budget.

The experience of a longtime copywriter, coupled with his current view from a marketing executive's chair, enables the author to bring a unique creative/marketing perspective to the guidance offered in this volume.

Mr. Nason is a native New Yorker, a graduate of Manhattan College and a veteran of the Army Signal Corps. He and his wife live in suburban Long Island with their three sons.

The secret of advertising

Each of us wears a Halloween mask all year long.

We have to, to keep our nerve endings hidden. To keep our hopes, and needs, and hangups, our fears and prides and prejudices, our irrationalities and our cry-buttons from hanging out for everyone to stare at.

Or step on.

We wear these shells to work, to lunch, to meetings, and to church. We always keep them handy for when friends drop in. And adjust them for *which* friends drop in.

It's this shell, whether it be button-down, Edwardian, or denim, that confuses a lot of us in advertising. If we're not careful, we find ourselves writing to the mannequin, instead of to the man inside, which often makes our ad cute but not convincing, beautiful but not believable, "swinging" but without substance.

Shell-talk forgets that inside each of us, no matter how old or young we are, is a person who is worried about his money, his age, his looks, his health, his happiness, his family, and whether people like him. Or hate him. Or worse, simply ignore him.

The secret of advertising, then, is to crack the shell, to talk to the man inside the man.

Simple it is, but easy it isn't.

It takes an uncommon understanding of people, great sensitivity and skill, and the discipline to use them every single time.

But it means the difference between an ad someone skips over and an ad someone reads all the way to the end.

Campbell-Ewald Company
Advertising

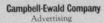

Courtesy of Campbell Ewald Company.

Preface

In 1977, when the first edition of this book made its appearance, the volume of U.S. advertising in measured media stood at $37.9 billion. By 1981 that figure had burgeoned beyond $60 billion. And the end is nowhere in sight. Those people with products or services to sell are becoming increasingly more reliant on advertising—in one form or another—to spread the word. Even general economic downturns have not had any appreciable effect on the enthusiasm with which business executives continue to embrace advertising.

In other words, there's still plenty of opportunity for a person bent on a career in advertising. And that will continue to be the case for as long as advertising remains the least expensive way for a seller to transmit a message to prospective buyers.

Not only is advertising widely accepted as a basic marketing tool, but fresh media sources are forever being sought. New magazines aimed at narrow market segments spring up like daffodils in the spring (while their larger-circulation brethren have their troubles). *Item:* The reverse side of supermarket checkout tapes, once blank, is now emblazoned with ad messages. *Item:* The ever-popular Yellow Pages have now unveiled a bright idea called "Gold Page Coupons." These multi-page inserts contain coupons, sponsored by participating merchants, which are redeemable at the retailer's place of business. *Item:* There was even a group urging the sale of advertising space on U.S. postage stamps, although Congress has wisely dismissed this proposal. And cable television now offers a whole new world of advertising possibilities.

Another trend that has taken place is advertising's accelerating dispersion from the fabled "canyons" of Madison Avenue. While the core of the business still remains concentrated in midtown New York, every year more and more advertising is being created in suburban communities, in Sunbelt cities and in those scenic locations that have become magnets for advertisers and agencies that once would never have considered leaving their roots and their peers in the old city centers.

For everyone interested in being a part of this business, this is surely good news. Once upon a time, serious advertising aspirants had to trek to New York or Chicago to learn their crafts and make their marks. Not anymore. Dallas, Atlanta, Boston, Denver, San Francisco and a dozen other cities today have thriving advertising communities. And hundreds of smaller towns and cities have more than creditable organizations where advertising is practiced on a high level.

This, of course, translates into a greater number of opportunities for beginners in every corner of the country. This second edition, updated and revised, is designed to meet this growing need. Its format and content are very basic. In its pages you will be introduced to many of the fundamental principles that go into the creation of effective advertising. These fundamentals are as applicable in Seattle and Cincinnati as in New York and Chicago; in small retail stores as in giant advertising agencies. Once grasped, they are yours to enlarge and enhance, with patience and practice, until the day comes when you are, indeed, the complete advertising professional, writing "the kind that works" with proven proficiency.

This book is intended to be your first step along that road.

Advertising-

How to write the kind that works

REVISED EDITION

Introduction

The word *copywriter* is a misnomer. Don't take it literally. At best, you'll spend only a portion of your time at a typewriter writing copy. The rest of the time? You'll be gathering information, checking the competition and thinking, thinking, thinking. Specifically:

• As a copywriter for a *corporation,* for example, you might very well spend half your time getting approvals for copy you have written—from the manufacturing and legal departments, for instance. Or you can eat up hours trying to coordinate your job with the photographers and production specialists (those involved with typesetting, engraving and printing) who take over after your work is completed.

• At an *advertising agency,* large chunks of your time will be devoured by meetings—with art directors, account executives, media and research people. You need facts and figures before you can "create" and you'll want to tap every possible source before beginning. And then there will be the time required (never enough) to "sell" your work to both your colleagues and the client.

• At a *retail store* you can spend tons of time just trying to get needed product information or tracking down department buyers for copy approvals.

• At a *radio or TV station* you might write scripts for local advertisers, edit others to conform to an announcer's delivery or to fit the time—or even develop promotional ideas to help the sales force drum up business.

• At a *newspaper* in the Retail Display Department, you will most likely also be "on the street" in face-to-face selling situations with retail accounts whose advertising it's your job to prepare.

So don't expect to be chained to your desk all day long. As a copywriter, you'll have to be an expert on collecting data from a wide variety of sources before assembling it in the most persuasive advertising possible. You'll often roam far afield in pursuit of this task.

THE BUCK STOPS WITH YOU

The word copywriter is also a misnomer because in many positions you're responsible for the entire, completed job, not just writing the copy. You're working as part of a "creative team." You'll spend hours deciding the most effective treatment for your advertisement. The tip-off on where the responsibility lies is evident in a crisis. If a job is late, the first place the production or traffic manager (who keeps all jobs on schedule) looks is at you, the copywriter. "Why is it late?" "What are you doing about it?" "How can we get it back on schedule?" You, the copywriter. The buck stops at your desk.

Working on a local newspaper, you'll often find you're not only the copywriter but also the account executive and "the artist" all rolled into one. But don't panic. The following chapters in this book are all designed to help you handle everything that comes your way.

What does a copywriter need to succeed? Heading the list is curiosity and imagination, followed quickly by tenacity and tact. Much the same as what is needed by a newspaper reporter. And you'll also need a grasp of grammar, spelling ability and a fair familiarity with a typewriter.

Beyond this, you must also be able to visualize the physical layout of your finished job. Often you must make everything happen yourself, including selection of the illustrations and arrangement of the elements (e.g. headline, pictures, etc.). When the time comes to write for radio and television, you'll be working with a whole new set of elements, including music and sound effects.

A copywriter should also possess patience and persistence. You should be prepared to chalk up part of your salary to frustration—especially when you're asked to rewrite the same piece of copy over and over again, until it comes out to your superior's satisfaction. Accept it as part of your work and not necessarily a reflection on your writing ability. You cannot possibly satisfy all the ad-approving authorities all the time. It's also important that you be extremely fussy about facts and figures: a "little" mistake could be very expensive—and very embarrassing.

HOW TO GET STARTED

If you want to be a (better) copywriter, here are a few steps to take before you start:

- Observe people (not just people like yourself either): college grads, blue-collar workers, all classes, all colors, all religions, jet-setters and go-getters. Everybody.

- Understand selling and merchandising: take a turn in a selling situation, watch how people react when making their purchasing decisions. You may be surprised.

- Study techniques: style, format, concepts. You need these basic tools before you start.

- Break out of routines: next vacation, fly to New York. Walk through Macy's department store, Gimbels, Bloomingdale's, Lord & Taylor, Tiffany. Look at their merchandising, advertising, customers. Keep your eyes and ears open. And your mouth, too! Ask questions. Next, take a bus to Bozeman, Montana. Talk to the person next to you along the way. Talk about anything: mostly politics and current events. What do they think? How do they live? What's important to them?

• Seek new viewpoints: when was the last time you looked at a copy of *Fortune? Ebony? Cosmopolitan?* How narrow are you? Men should look at ads in women's magazines and vice versa. Study the ads. Broaden your base. See the styles, the concepts, the layouts, the ideas.

As a copywriter you are a vital cog in the total marketing effort discussed in the next chapter. The power you have as a communicator will one day astound you. Remember not to get so tied down with deadlines that you forget to stroll through the factory (or your client's factory), or occasionally visit a point of sale. You'll see what a valuable contribution you are making toward the marketing goals, toward making jobs available, toward a better standard of living, toward making it all happen.

Or even more dramatic, go to the railroad siding that serves your factory and watch the boxcars roll out, brimming with the products that you have helped create a market for. The fact that you played a part in all this will help make the scene all the more impressive to you.

Or travel down to the selling floor in your department store to see the shoppers as they come streaming in for those Red Tag Day specials in response to your ad in last night's paper.

Or, if you're working for a nonprofit organization, see how the membership has swelled, or count the bags of mail requesting the new pamphlet your last ad offered.

Then you'll go back to your typewriter with renewed enthusiasm, knowing that you, a copywriter, can help accomplish great things!

Organization
and relationships

2

Advertising is a team effort. It's like a symphony orchestra in which a variety of talents have to play in tune for the end result to be anything you expect. It takes a high degree of coordination between writers, art directors, account executives, media planners, research specialists, traffic and production people, photographers, artists, printers, engravers (or camera crews, directors, film editors and a retinue of others if you're in TV). And this barely scratches the surface. A bewildering array of people are involved as an ad or commercial proceeds from conception to the final glittering result you see in *Better Homes and Gardens* or on the late news. If all the gears don't mesh, you're in trouble. Everything grinds to a halt. Teamwork is the only answer. What's the writer's role in all this? Right smack in the center of things.

Let's take a look now at some of the ways the advertising industry is organized to make things happen smoothly—most of the time, anyway. We'll begin with a glimpse inside probably the best-oiled machine of all, the large advertising agency.

5

ADVERTISING AGENCIES

An advertising agency is simply an outside organization that offers specialists in planning, creating and making the most appropriate (most efficient) media selection for this advertising. The key word is "specialists." This means people who do this full time for a variety of different advertisers. They're therefore able to bring a depth of experience to the job that no advertiser is able to provide by himself. One of those specialists is you, the copywriter.

How does an ad agency work? What makes it tick? Since it plays such an important role in the business, you should have an idea of how it's structured and how it performs.

Once an account is awarded to an advertising agency, the agency assigns an account executive who will serve as the agency's representative on the account. Most of a client's dealings with the agency will be through him or her. In smaller agencies, one of the agency principals will often serve in this role. The account representative is the conduit through which information is transmitted to the agency and who, in turn, provides the client company with the benefit of the agency's experience in creating ads, selecting media and planning campaigns. Account executives must have many talents. They have to combine the skills of a reporter (to communicate information completely and accurately), a salesman (to convince the advertiser that the agency's ads are thoughtfully conceived and well-executed—because sometimes everyone doesn't see eye to eye on this) and a manager (to make sure the agency's services and the client's needs are always coordinated). They have to have a working knowledge of media, production and research. They must be able to keep cool, look confident and be diplomatic. Good to have around!

At the agency, each account executive is wired in to the full range of agency services. Creative is probably the most important. The account executive works closely with the copywriter and art director who have been assigned to develop the ads. Each of these people has superiors, all the way up to the president of the agency. This varies from agency to agency. When a new client arrives at an agency, he will generally request a rundown of the organization.

While the primary contact between a client and the agency

Della Femina, Travisano & Partners Inc.
625 MADISON AVENUE, NEW YORK, NEW YORK 10022

WORK REQUISITION

Client _____ Date _____ Job No. _____

● Product _____ Caption _____

Account Executive _____ _____

INSTRUCTIONS

CREATIVE TEAM: _____ COPY _____ ART _____

PUBLICATIONS	ISSUE DATE	SPACE, COLOR (NOTE IF BLEED)	SIZE SPECIFICATIONS (WIDTH X DEPTH)	(SAFETY)	SCREEN	CLOSING

● Production Estimate Needed _____ Copy Due _____ Layout Due _____

Order Space _____ Tentative _____ Mechanical Due _____

TRAFFIC

WORK REQUISITION FORM: In an advertising agency, each specific writing assignment is authorized on a form like this. Copies go to the Copywriter, Art Director, Account Executive, as well as to the Media, Production and Traffic departments. Such internal coordination and control is essential to avoid errors. *Courtesy DellaFemina, Travisano & Partners Inc.*

is the account executive, this does not preclude contact with others involved in the business. Good clients make it a point to get to know people like you who are intimately connected with their advertising. All of these meetings give you abundant opportunity to learn a little more about the product—and a little first-hand familiarity with the client can't hurt should you get a chance to sell him on your ideas later on! From a client's point of view, these contacts serve to reassure him that his account is in good hands, that good people are looking after his interests.

Creative development

The normal operating procedure with a client runs something like this. At the very outset, those people who are most familiar with the production and/or the marketing of the product or service to be advertised are brought together. Detailed discussion on the specific nature of the target audience—based on experience, of course, and current research, if available—is also an essential ingredient of these preliminary conversations.

The agency team then digests all this information and returns with a Unique Selling Proposition (see Chapter 4). The copywriter plays a vital role in this. Only when both agency and client agree can actual creative work start.

The next step is development of advertising layouts and copy (see Work Requisition, p. 7), and the drafting of a media plan. These two operations are performed separately but concurrently. On one hand, it is essential for the copywriter to know where his or her ads will be appearing (see Chapter 3), while on the other hand, the nature of the sales message or creative execution might serve to influence the media selection.

The advertising layouts and the media proposal are then presented to the client for approval. This is always an exhilarating time. If you've developed advertising that the client expects, then your job is easier. But is this what he's paying for? Doesn't he deserve better? The easy way is not the better way at all. This is the challenge that creative agency people must grapple with. Clients like "safe" advertising because it's probably close to what the competition is doing. In similarity there is comfort. Clients often have another weakness: being too close to their products, they fail to see how everyone can't be as fascinated in the subject

Death of an idea:

It's so easy to say no to it.

It's so understandable to want to fix it and make it more conventional and familiar.

It's so reassuring to take the alarming part out of it and smooth the rough edges. And sand-paper it to death.

Oscar Wilde put it this way: "An idea that isn't danger-ous is hardly worth calling an idea at all."

It's the shocking part, the frightening part, the unknown element that makes an idea an idea in the first place. If you feel comfortable with it from the very first, take another look.

It's probably not an idea.

J. Walter Thompson Company

COPYWRITERS MUST LEARN to explain their position . . . and to bounce back fast when they fail to persuade others of the merit of their ideas. *Courtesy J. Walter Thompson Company.*

as they are. The agency, on the other hand, knows otherwise. In fact, breaking down the apathy barrier is one of the hardest jobs of any ad or commercial. So you normally enter one of these "presentations" knowing that you've taken the harder road but it's what's best for the client. All you've got to do now is convince him of that!

Good clients realize the most important contribution an agency can make comes from its objective viewpoint, its ability to weigh the *realities* of the marketplace. No fantasies allowed! Just hard-nosed conclusions that will give a client the best chance of success in that market. The very distance of an agency from a product (at least compared to the client) forces it to look at things from the consumer's point of view, without rose-colored glasses. And that's a very realistic place to be for anyone who's trying to sell anything. Customers can fool you. Handle them with care!

Finishing the job

When the layouts and the copy have been approved and everybody's in agreement where the ads will appear, the next step is setting the type, taking the photographs or ordering the artwork and then making an "engraving" for shipment to the newspaper. (Many newspapers are printed by the "offset" method rather than the traditional "letterpress," which means they need "repro material" or "slicks" rather than "engravings." And if half-tones are involved, the paper may require "film" for reproduction. But this is a technical distinction that will be resolved by your agency without affecting you.)

The advertiser gets a chance to see and to approve each ad as it proceeds along the way. The agency assumes responsibility for getting the material to the publisher before "closing date." This may be only a few days in advance, in the case of newspapers, or several months for certain magazines.

Agency compensation

Who pays for the services of an advertising agency? Not necessarily the advertiser. Advertising agencies, much like insurance brokers or travel agents, are paid by a third party to the transaction. In this case, the media where the advertising is placed: newspapers, magazines, radio, television, billboards, or whatever.

Here's how it works. If an advertiser goes to a newspaper with an ad for a full page, the newspaper will charge him the published rate for a full-page ad. Let's say it's $1,000. That means a bill for $1,000 payable at the end of the month. However if that same ad is brought to the same newspaper by an advertising agency, the agency pays at a rate 15% less—in this case $850. The agency then turns around and sends the advertiser a bill for $1,000. So in effect an advertiser pays no more than before but has availed himself of expert counsel in the creation of his advertising. This is called the 15% agency commission and has been traditional in advertising for over 100 years, dating back to the time when newspapers recognized the revenue opportunities in advertising and were anxious to compensate the advertising "agents" who solicited and wrote ads and steered business their way.

Remember that the agency has to pay salaries, rent, utilities and all kinds of other overhead from this 15% commission, so it doesn't represent pure profit. In fact, a typical ad agency net profit hovers somewhere around 1%.

After the ad runs, the publisher will bill the agency for the price of the space, less the 15% commission, of course. The agency then bills the client for the full price of the space (that is, including the 15%) agreed on earlier. There are also discounts to be gained for prompt payment. The agency will normally try to take advantage of these discounts and then pass along the savings to the client. However, if clients don't get in the habit of then paying bills promptly to the agency, the agency stops tying up its cash this way.

Local rates

However, ad agency compensation isn't that simple. Local advertisers are often granted special "local rates" for their advertising. (A company that only does business in the community served by the newspaper would usually qualify as a local advertiser. A lumber yard would probably warrant local-advertiser status and rates; a paint company in town that distributes in a much wider area probably would not.) These local rates are lower than the "national" rates paid by an advertising agency for the same space. So it's quite possible that an advertiser might be able to earn a break in the rates and pay only $900 for the same space that your agency would pay $1,000 for.

What the 15% commission buys

As a general rule, the basic agency services are included in the 15% commission the agency earns from the media. This includes all the creative work, marketing counsel, campaign planning and media recommendations. Sometimes, depending on the size of an account, its growth potential or special relationship with the agency, it may get more than this. But seldom less. In most cases the chief extra charges will be in the "production" services provided by suppliers outside the agency: photography, artwork, typesetting and engraving (or "film") are the principal costs. If the advertising is broadcast on radio or television, extra costs will come from a whole raft of technicians, talent, props and studio charges. These costs are billed to the agency, which in turn sends the bill to the client. Traditionally, the agency adds its commission, too. Only now you start hearing the number 17.65% instead of 15%. The reason is simple math. An artwork charge of, let's say, $85 must be increased by 17.65% to bring it up to $100. Why $100? Because 15% of $100 is $15, which when subtracted from $100 leaves $85. So 17.65% going up is the same as 15% coming down—in effect, the agency remuneration remains constant. Such anticipated production costs are normally figured separately and added to the cost of media space in the proposed budget.

As a writer in an advertising agency, you'll probably enjoy more variety than you will anywhere else. You're likely to be writing ads for an instant coffee today and an airline tomorrow. You'll normally be assigned to several different accounts and even these will change from year to year. But the variety of challenges you'll face will probably sharpen your writing skills. You'll see a job through from start to finish, too. If a commercial has to be shot in an exotic location or a Hollywood studio, you'll often be there for the shooting. (But more often, the "location" will be in a local studio, so don't get your hopes up.) It's fun, but also demanding.

How to pick an agency

Maybe you're a businessman who's been able to write your own advertising up to now. But maybe you think it's about time you got some help so that you can concentrate on other aspects of your business. If this is the case and you're thinking about hiring an advertising agency, here are some considerations that might be valuable to you.

• Choose your agency carefully. There are probably a number of small advertising agencies in your town, certainly in the nearest large city. Talk to your fellow businessmen, ask the Chamber of Commerce or simply look in the Yellow Pages. Talk to several agencies. Ask to see what they've done for others. Meet some of the people who would be responsible for your advertising. Are you comfortable with them? Do you feel confident in them? Do they seem to be on the same wavelength as you? It might also be a good idea to check with some of their present accounts to see if the agency's clients are satisfied with the caliber of the people and the quality of the work. And always check with the Better Business Bureau. If an agency is a member of the American Association of Advertising Agencies (the 4-As to those in the business), it's a good sign that the agency is organized in a professional manner. To find out, contact the 4-As' office in New York. (See p. 210 for the address.)

• Let your hair down as much as possible. Once you select an agency, start to think of the people there as part of the family. To do their job successfully, they have to be very close to you, virtually an extension of your business. Let them know all about your business (at least in a general way, not necessarily with your latest balance sheet). They should be told your sales records, what kinds of goods or services are more profitable to sell than others, what special sales techniques you've tried (whether or not they've been successful) and what your plans are for the future—not only this month or this year but five years down the road.

• Get your money's worth. If you consider advertising as merely a device to move merchandise from point A (your store) to point B (the buyer), you're not realizing the agency's potential. Advertising can do more than sell a rack of men's suits or a carload of wood paneling. If you view advertising as a means of building a continuing confidence in you and your business, exemplified by whatever is featured in the various ads, then the horizon is unlimited. Those who see advertising as nothing more than a necessary evil will probably begrudge their agency access to information that would allow it to advance beyond the "curtains for sale" stage. There will be no opportunity for the agency to "position" your business so that people think of you when they need a certain product or service, whether they've just seen your ad in the paper or not. Those who properly understand the role of advertising know that it is an investment that has immediate as well as long-range goals. When you understand advertising this way, you will not hesitate to share both your experiences and your plans with your agency, and you will surely get the most mileage from the money you apply to advertising.

To repeat, an agency can be of maximum help only if it is allowed to know a great deal about your business: where it's been, how it got where it is today and where you want to be in the years ahead. Be frank. Treat your agency like a good friend.

Do you need an agency? That depends on how important advertising is to your business. Can you afford an agency? The cost is modest when you consider the work it does for you. Will an advertising agency be interested in your business? Yes, if it figures it can make a fair profit in the arrangement; no, if it can't. You're in business, the same as an advertising agency, and neither of you can be expected to work for charity. Sometimes a monthly fee is added on to make your account profitable to an agency. Talk it over. Be honest. There's a good chance you'll be able to reach an agreement.

RETAIL ADVERTISING

A large department store or chain headquarters can easily keep many full-time copywriters on its own payroll. Such in-house staffing by the store itself gives a copywriter greater intimacy with the many products to be advertised, more control of the store's style of advertising (the image factor) and better coordination with the individual store buyers who approve the ads. In-store advertising operations also permit greater deadline controls and more flexibility with the layout artists, who often are just across the aisle from the copywriters.

This kind of ability to switch gears quickly is absolutely essential in the retail field. A shipment doesn't arrive when expected. A "special" sells out faster than planned (congratulations!). A buyer suddenly receives a carload of imported rugs that weren't due until next week. In the madcap retail world, anything can happen—and usually does. You've got to be ready to shift back and forth at a moment's notice. You can't afford to be sensitive. Or a prima donna. Not in retail! With few exceptions, this hectic pace has usually held back any workable arrangement between a department store and an advertising agency.

The workload, too, is a factor that has led department stores to be do-it-yourselfers. A department store generates a great volume of advertising that usually runs just once. An agency simply isn't geared to make a profit on this kind of business. Campaign planning, long-term programs, carefully crafted ads or commercials that have a long running life in national magazines and network television–this is the meat and potatoes of an ad agency. It's normally not the kind of work required by a department store.

A copywriter in the department store situation quickly learns to be very versatile. Besides those ads for tomorrow's newspaper, you'll likely be writing copy for counter cards, rack headers, catalogs, mailing pieces of all kinds, handouts—you name it. And fast! The retail scene has proven to be an excellent training ground for generations of copywriters. You learn to avoid getting flustered, to keep your cool, to work with the pressure of deadlines. It's an experience for which many writers who move on to fame and fortune in the ad agency business are forever grateful.

NEWSPAPER AD DEPARTMENTS

Most newspaper ads come either from major local advertisers (food, department or discount chains) or are part of national brand campaigns. Invariably, this advertising comes to the newspaper already prepared, ready to run. The newspaper makeup man simply takes this material, inserts it in position on the page and that's that.

Still, there are many local businesses with no agency affiliation that need assistance on the spot. This is where the newspaper space salesman needs to be very versatile: sometimes the best way to bring in new advertisers is by helping a retailer prepare his advertising. This often means the space salesman must be ready to write an ad and lay it out, too. Sometimes artwork is made available by branded products that can be included in the ad. Another possible source of artwork for ads is the national association that the businessman might belong to (there's one for virtually every type of business). In any event, the salesman who can give local advertisers a hand in preparing their ads is more likely to bring in the business. Encourage them. Urge them. Show them. The easier it's made, the more likely the store will take the plunge.

This kind of copywriting experience also offers some real face-to-face sales contact, too. And that's always a valuable lesson for a writer. This kind of opportunity exists at most papers, large and small, big-city dailies as well as small-town weeklies. It may not always be glamorous (nothing *is*) but it has the special virtue of bringing the writer close to the point of sale, which is always a rewarding experience.

Other major media also have advertising departments to service their clients.

ONE-PERSON ORGANIZATIONS

Although the jack-of-all-trades is becoming more and more a rarity, he or she is still holding on strong in certain quarters.

• One person can be an advertising agency. Yes, you could be your own advertising agency, using free-lance specialists for everything you can't do personally yourself—perhaps the artwork, photography or even the copywriting on occasion. Free-lance specialists are not on your permanent payroll. You merely call them at home or at their studios and they do whatever you need done for your client on a piecework basis.

• A small manufacturing corporation might have one person responsible for doing much of the writing of the company's literature while coordinating the company's advertising with an outside advertising agency.

• An advertising "organization" can be one person responsible for advertising for a retail store. You work directly with the media, whether it's the newspaper space sales representative or the local radio or TV time sales rep.

• Very small local radio stations and weekly newspapers may have one person who "minds the store," providing local merchants with help and guidance in preparing ads. A basic familiarity with advertising techniques, coupled with the special knowledge of the media where you work, is often all that is needed to bring in business. Local enterprises want to advertise with you but don't know how to begin. That's where you come in.

MARKETING

One of the most confusing things about advertising for some people is its relationship to marketing, merchandising and public relations. So let's try to pull them apart and analyze them as simply as possible.

Marketing is the total management effort to sell products, services or ideas successfully. Marketing is not limited to just the use of advertising: many other ingredients are necessary for a successful marketing effort. Many corporations have a Marketing Director whose responsibilities can include, but are not limited to, pricing (is it competitively priced?), distribution (is it sufficiently available?), sales policies (are our discounts and other allowances satisfactory?), credit policy (are our terms equal to what the competition is offering?), packaging (does it break when shipped?). And somewhere along the way the marketing department must make certain the advertising efforts are generating an urge to buy.

All or any of these factors can affect the success of a marketing program, along with others that could be peculiar to just a specific product. As you can see, advertising is only one part of the marketing "mix." When the total mix is correct, success usually is much more likely. Unless, of course, you are trying to sell horseshoes in New York City or overcoats in Miami.

Advertising, then, is one of the communication tools in the marketing mix. The other formalized communication tool is public relations. Also important is informal communication: word-of-mouth advertising by sales personnel or by present users of the product.

It follows that you can have a great advertising campaign but still have product failure. Merely reread the other items necessary for a successful marketing effort. Advertising should not be made to take the full brunt of a marketing effort that fails (nor full credit if it succeeds), and most Marketing Directors realize this. The successful Marketing Director is like a master chef, standing by a busy stove making sure there are no slip-ups. The Advertising Manager in most corporations reports to the Marketing Director.

So much for the "fit" of where marketing and advertising belong in the management apparatus that brings products to market.

MERCHANDISING

Merchandising is bringing together all the timely variables at "the moment of truth": the decision to buy or not buy. Is the product or service priced properly? Is the product properly designed for the season? Is it sold properly, including the image the seller wants projected? Is the product displayed properly?

A department store moved its major appliance department from the third to the first floor to get more traffic for this high-ticket item. The store's management felt it was smart merchandising to change the product's display location. Ever notice how magazines and other impulse items are placed near the supermarket checkout? That's no accident, just good merchandising. Many of the larger local stores, both independent and chain, have Merchandise Managers on their staffs.

PUBLIC RELATIONS

Public relations (PR) means many things to many people. The relationship between advertising and PR seems confused at first, but they are relatively simple to distinguish. In a corporate organization the public relations staff can be sitting just across the aisle from the advertising staff, so it is doubly important that you realize their relationship.

Public relations is all-encompassing. Most of the time it will consist of all the various ways and means of presenting the company to the public. Even advertising can be brought into play to bring added support to the total public relations program of a company or organization (see p. 20). Both PR people and advertising people are communicators. They simply use different tools: publicity releases (which may or may not be used by the various media: it's a very chancy business), speakers' bureaus, open house events, arrangements for company spokesmen to appear on TV or radio talk shows or to be interviewed for news stories, providing feature material for publications (mostly of a general editorial nature, but always weaving in the company's point of view or products). For important events the public relations people will arrange conferences, inviting key media and providing a "kit" containing all the pertinent information and photographs for the editors and reporters to take back to the office to help them write the story.

For maximum effect tight-knit coordination between paid-for publicity (advertising) and free publicity (through public relations efforts) is important. A good example is the communications blitz drummed up each year by Detroit when it comes time to roll out the new car models. Not only does the manufacturer invest heavily in paid advertising but at the same time the PR staff is busy sending out news releases and photographs to the media about the new models. They hope these publicity releases will capture free space in the news and feature columns of local newspapers and magazines, perhaps even getting TV or radio time.

For maximum impact, your PR activity should be carefully coordinated with the appearance of your paid advertising investment.

Why we take care of our trees.

If you were a farmer whose only crop had a 50 year growing cycle, you'd take very good care of it, right? Well, we are that farmer. Our crop takes 50 years, on average, to reach maturity.

That's why we plant up to six seedlings for every tree we harvest, why we nurture them, prune them, thin them, protect them from insects, disease and fire.

That's why we continually explore new forest management techniques that promise more trees per acre, and new manufacturing processes that promise more wood and paper per tree.

That's why we increasingly use what once was wasted, either to make products like yeast, chunk bark and particleboard, or to generate energy.

It's a matter of self-interest, finally. Only by managing our trees prudently can we provide the jobs, products and profits we all need and the forests we all love.

 Boise Cascade Corporation
Wood and paper for today, trees for tomorrow.

"PUBLIC RELATIONS ADVERTISING" in action. A company draws attention to its reforestation programs that replace the trees that are cut down. *Courtesy Boise Cascade Corporation.*

LIVING WITH YOUR ARTIST

Since advertising is a visual medium (aside from radio) and you're a writer, an art director or artist plays an important role in your work. Traditionally, most advertising concepts have originated with copywriters. Although there are more and more concept-creating art directors sprouting up in ad agencies, the writer remains the starting point for most new advertising—a fact that is recognized without minimizing the contribution of the art professional, who will give form and shape to an idea that is often nothing more than a typed sheet accompanied by a doodle. The finished ad is a joint effort by two creative people.

However, when two creative people get together, sparks often fly. This is good. The idea is to make sure the sparks ignite a sensational layout and are not merely the wasted result of two egos clashing. It's usually up to you, as the copywriter, to make sure this partnership works. Feed the artist your words and ideas, explain fully the objective you're trying to achieve, give him some indication of the way you see things and then step back and let the artist do his thing. He's not merely a technician who can draw, any more than you're merely a technician who can write.

The fact remains, however, that you're probably closer to the product and the problem than the artist and therefore in a better position to know what is "right." If your artist is going off on a tangent, say so. Be fair but firm. At the same time, always keep an open mind about new and better ways to present your original idea.

The more you and your artist become a "team," the more productive you'll be—both of you. Cooperation is better than confrontation. Become friends. Share ideas. Get his or her creative juices flowing and the results will make you both happy. It's worth the effort.

LIVING WITH YOUR CLIENT

There's one other relationship that you should never put very far out of your mind. That's the one you must establish with your "client." Normally, that refers to the company (or person within that company) for whom you're creating advertising. Be careful. Be thorough. Be firm. People respect those with the courage of their convictions. But also observe a little common sense. The following rules might help you live and laugh another day:

- The client pays the bills.

- Try to persuade him your ad has merit and will be effective.

- Don't push too hard. After all, there are few absolute answers in this business.

- Remember, there is always another day—the client may think the rejected idea is great then!

- Sometimes you'll never know who the client really listens to for advertising advice. Maybe it's not you at all, really. Maybe he takes everything home to show the family!

- If you can't live with the client, something is going to give. Guess which side will win?

- Advertising is a subjective art, remember?

- Before you lose a client, be sure you can afford to!

LIVING WITH YOUR FRIENDS

Because advertising is so highly visible, it offers a very inviting target. Some of the critics of this $60-billion-plus industry may even be your own friends. Various people question the whole idea of using psychology and persuasion in advertising communication. "Advertising makes people buy things they don't need" is a familiar charge. So are these: "Advertising increases a product's cost," "Advertising is wasteful," and "Advertising limits competition."

It's not the purpose of this book to respond to this kind of shallow swipe or to become too deeply involved in the philosophical aspects of advertising. However, since the questions are raised periodically, you should know that such charges are based more on appearances than reality, more on emotion than fact. You have no reason to be defensive.

First of all, an advertising copywriter has no monopoly on

applying psychology and persuasion in his or her daily work. You're in good company. Lawyers, educators and religious leaders are others who use the same tools of the trade. The idea of sizing up an audience and then selecting and presenting facts in the most persuasive fashion is a skill practiced by many professions.

As far as making people buy things they don't need—who's to say what people "need"? All anyone really needs is food, shelter and a warm fire. Everything else simply contributes to making our lives more pleasant. As long as consumers enjoy free choice in a competitive society, no one can make them do what they don't want to do. Advertising is no exception.

It's true that advertising is a business expense and someone's going to pay for it. Certainly there are pennies in each tube of toothpaste to help pay for the advertising. But without advertising constantly cultivating markets for these products, mass-production methods would be virtually impossible. And who's to say how much more that toothpaste or car would cost if it could not be manufactured by high-speed assembly made necessary because advertising increased demand?

Products, or companies, that engage in "wasteful" advertising normally aren't around very long. Should we try to make our current advertising practices more efficient? Certainly. That's every copywriter's challenge and one reason for this book. Another definition of "wasteful advertising" refers to promotion of an endless number of products and models that seem to accomplish the same thing. Since white towels will dry you as well as any others, why offer the others? Simply because people have rational and emotional sides. Their rational side knows that white does the job but their emotional needs call for color. Who's to say they're wrong? Not you.

Advertising limits competition? Far from it. Advertising keeps the competitive fires burning. Every consumer should be glad to see the range of choices—in quality as well as in price— that appear in advertising. Just look at how the advertising for foreign autos gave the American public another choice—one that they apparently wanted, if you measure the inroads foreign cars have made on the American market.

To keep the record straight, it must be acknowledged that there is a certain amount of deceptive advertising. No excuse can, or should, be made for such practices. Despite the fact that such acts are invariably exceptions, they tend to tarnish the entire industry. Sad but true. Those found guilty are prosecuted under existing laws. Mandatory corrective advertising is becoming more common. But the highest price an offender pays is loss of reputation. Once deceived, customers rarely return.

This, then, is the most important relationship of all: that between advertiser and customer. As a copywriter, your role in strengthening this link cannot be overstated.

The medium and your message

3

As a copywriter it's important to have a clear understanding of the medium in which your efforts will appear. Often the limitations of a specific medium will have a direct bearing on how you approach your work. The success of your efforts will depend on your grasp of how the medium works. An obvious example. when writing for outdoor billboards, it's important to be brief. But newspapers, radio, magazines and television all have different ways of relating to their audiences. It's important you understand the distinction.

You should also know enough about the media to understand the role they can play in the success or failure of your efforts. The selection of media, scheduling the appearances of the advertising, even the placement of the ad within a paper or the air time of a commercial—these are all often as crucial as what the advertising message itself says. For example, the right message on the wrong TV program (imagine a Geritol commercial on a kiddie cartoon show!) is much like the proverbial tree falling in the uninhabited forest, with no one around to hear the noise it

25

makes. There must be a tight, right fit between the medium and your message. A copywriter who doesn't have a basic appreciation of the media never fully perceives his place in the picture and consequently operates with one hand tied. Learn a little about the media. Don't handicap yourself.

MEDIA EFFICIENCY

There are literally thousands of different newspapers, magazines and radio and televison stations, each clamoring for attention and each seemingly able to make a case for a position on the media list. More and more, computers have been enlisted (at least by ad agencies) to sort out the bewildering maze of figures supplied by the various media to espouse their cause.

The basic question to be answered is this: which media offer the most efficient means to take your message to your target audience? This is commonly stated in a figure called "cost per thousand" (the cost of reaching a thousand readers or viewers), which gives the industry a simple yet useful basis of comparison. This figure is quickly calculated by dividing the cost of the unit of advertising by the circulation (of a newspaper or magazine) or the audience (of a television or radio time period) and then multiplying this number by 1000. However, even though this yardstick is the most common and most convenient, each medium conducts continuing studies of the nature of its audience.

This type of in-depth research is no longer confined to the media themselves. Syndicated—or shared—research also provides valuable input. This is purchased from impartial outside organizations that carefully study the exact audience composition above and beyond simple circulation figures. Some magazines have more "pass along" readership than others—for example, all those magazines that you browse through while waiting for the dentist or the barber to call your turn. Some get thumbed-through quickly while others are read carefully. Then there are those magazines read by the whole family, which are quite distinct from those read by, let's say, sports car buffs.

However, buying based only on the total number of readers, viewers or listeners is rarely the most economical, efficient, beneficial or profitable way. Buying media time or space must go beyond

"Boys' Life is a sharp media buy"

"Uncle Henry"/Henry Baer, President, Schrade Cutlery Corp., Ellenville, New York

Henry Baer, President of Schrade Cutlery, says "We think Boys' Life is a sharp media buy—and at Schrade, sharpness is our business.

"We know how important durability and top construction are in a knife, and boys realize this too.

"Boys can also appreciate the beauty of a Schrade knife, along with its toughness and our unique guarantee. Whether for camping, hiking or fishing, boys want a knife they can depend on and Schrade knives meet their needs.

"In the last four years, our ads for Schrade have established a place for us in the Boys' Life market. We are selling knives today and also building a market for the future as these customers keep coming back for Schrade quality."

Discover the power of Boys' Life and increase your sales as Schrade did. For more information, call Bob Goldsmith, Marketing Director, at (212) 532-0985 or contact your local Boys' Life sales rep.

When the male youth market is your target audience, you can't miss with

BOYS' LIFE
THE MAGAZINE FOR ALL BOYS
Published by the
Boy Scouts of America

MEDIA EFFICIENCY means making sure your advertising is put before your likeliest prospects with the very least amount of "waste" audience. *Courtesy Boys' Life. Photo Courtesy Mr. Ed Haas.*

just the "numbers game" of circulation figures or the "ratings game" so popular with TV and radio stations. Numbers should be considered only in relation to the exact nature and type of audience. A media "buy" should give ample weight to demographics, life-styles and the best potential consumer. This is particularly necessary as media costs continue to soar. Needless to say, this type of data has been the hardest part to computerize for more sophisticated media-buying operations.

What it all boils down to is this: the final decisions surely take all the mathematical calculations into account but nothing can replace the experience and judgment of a seasoned media expert.

If you're a local retail advertiser, you'll find that the media mix is usually far less complicated to develop (due to limited budgets and trade area) than it is for a national advertiser. Most retail stores and services depend on some combination of newspapers and radio, sometimes TV and possibly direct mail, outdoor and transit advertising too. Advertising specialties (for example, matchbook covers) also occasionally find a way into the budget, as do other media, including directories. Point-of-purchase (POP) displays usually are supplied free by the manufacturers.

LOOKING AT NEWSPAPERS

Newspapers continue to get the lion's share of total advertising dollars. This is easily seen when you thumb through the local daily newspaper on the Wednesday or Thursday "food days." Full page after full page of supermarket advertising, every week. Then come page after page of department store, chain variety and discount store ads, both midweek and on Sundays. It all puts newspapers ahead of TV in total dollars spent for advertising. Newspaper size may vary from the "standard-size" paper, six to eight columns wide, to a smaller tabloid size, normally five columns wide.

Newspaper space is relatively easy for an advertiser to buy, particularly since so many cities have become one-paper towns. Often, if there is a morning and evening paper, they're owned by the same management: sometimes "combination rates" are available if your ad is in both papers. However, keep a sharp eye on your target audience when a media buyer proposes this combination. Why? Because the morning paper usually has a heavy following of businessmen on their way to work, while the evening newspaper normally dominates home and family reader-ship. Totally different audiences! If your advertising is aimed at both, fine. If not, the combination rate might not be a bargain.

Newspapers serve a general mixture of readers, with great variations of age, educational level, income, interests and life-style. For this reason effective media buyers must fine-tune their thinking when buying newspaper space.

Unlike the newspaper's classified ads, display advertising lets you mix both type and artwork together. It's usually sold by inches deep per columns wide; rates are readily available in the newspaper's rate card, the *Ayer Directory of Publications* or in the *Standard Rate & Data* for newspapers.

Ad placement

Fine-tuning can include answering such questions as the following: Are you advertising on the right days? Are you familiar with the major employers' paydays in town? Do you watch for school holidays, when children are available for shopping trips? When are the three-day weekends?

Similarly, media buyers consider sectionalized parts of the newspaper for better placement of your advertising message, in-cluding the women's page, society page, homemaker's section, financial section or real estate section, rather than settling for run of the paper (ROP) positions. A shoe store might find it very profitable to advertise in the entertainment section if research showed that women who read the entertainment page are ex-tremely fashion-conscious, particularly about shoes! Intelligent placement of your advertising message within the paper can in-crease its effectiveness.

"Next to reading matter" is a position that helps keep your message from being buried in a corner under three other ads, or worse. Some newspapers charge extra for this preference. Others will try to accommodate the advertiser—if requested.

"Full position" in a newspaper can usually be purchased to assure that your ad will have reading matter on two sides of it.

GOOD HOUSEKEEPING®

THE MAGAZINE AMERICA LIVES BY

CONTENTS

page 114   page 116   page 140

NOVEL

Reach for the Dawn ....Elisabeth Ogilvie 173

SHORT STORIES

A View from the Heart ....Rosamunde Pilcher 124
Fairy Tale *(short short)* ....Daphne du Maurier 138

ARTICLES & FEATURES

Inflation-Fighter: Money-Gram 34
My Problem: I Married Him and Got His Whole Family 36
Children's Page ....Joan Walsh Anglund 50
Advice to Teens ....Abigail Van Buren 52
The Triplets Who Found Each Other ....Phyllis Battelle 74
Jane Monell's Gift to Working
    Mothers-to-Be ....Sally Wendkos Olds 90
Three Women Who Dared ......Charles Kuntzleman with Lyn Cryderman 111
The Guide to Love ....Grace Shirley 112
Shirley Temple: Her Movies, Her Life ....Joseph N. Bell 114
The Complete Book of
    Plastic Surgery ....V. Michael Hogan, M.D., with Ruth Winter 126

DEPARTMENTS

Letters 1c
Editor's Notebook 4
Light Housekeeping 20
Speaker for the House ....Charlotte Montgomery 28
Etiquette for Every Day ....Elizabeth L. Post 42
Family Doctor ....Alan E. Nourse, M.D. 66
What's New! ....Ann Elkins 72
Dr. Joyce Brothers Answers Your Questions 102

FOOD

Susan Learns to Make the Best Chocolate Fudge 48
Food Editor's Tips ....Mildred Ying 70
30-Minute Entrée: Franks and Spaghetti 84
Favorites from Our Dining Room: Valentine Sugar Cookies 106
The Chicken Cookbook 140
Festive Desserts for February 14th 210
Fresh Ideas for Oranges 170
Deliciously Different Cheese Ideas 241

BEAUTY

Makeover #40: The Slimming Look 62
Your Beauty Notebook 98
25 Fresh New Hairdos 116

CONTINUED ON PAGE 10

PREMIUM POSITIONS such as this high-readership spot adjacent to a magazine's table of contents are much in demand by advertisers, and are priced accordingly. *Courtesy CPC International and Good Housekeeping.*

Such a position also means forcing your message closer to the top of the newspaper page for more attention.

Other requested positions in a newspaper bring forth a wrath of disagreement. Some advertisers feel they want their ad "above the fold" in a standard size paper. Others feel a right-hand page draws more attention and readership than a left-hand page. "Right, above the fold, next to reading matter," is the way some advertisers insist their ads must run.

When your ad runs a full page, you don't have to worry about the clutter of other ads crowding your message. This is very effective but also very expensive. Can less than a full-page ad get more impact than you might expect? Yes, if it's designed properly. Or you can be lucky and find your ad sharing a page with a big story that holds a reader's attention longer than usual and gives your ad more chance to be seen.

Small space

Depending on their own individual policies, some newspapers will let advertisers strip out the bottom of a page. To do this, the media buyer buys an ad the maximum width of the page (all columns across) by one to five inches deep. Sometimes there's a minimum depth imposed by the newspaper; some newspapers will even let you strip out the top of a page! This allows your ad to appear to dominate the page without making a large investment.

Another bright idea for small budgets is to consider buying one single column width from top to bottom. Or if the budget allows, this can be repeated twice on the same page by skipping a few columns between the ads. This will help avoid having your message buried on the page! Excellent use of the single-column technique was shown by a retail lighting fixture store which featured artwork of a hanging lamp descending all the way down one column, where the ad copy appeared at the very bottom.

Using the reverse technique (white on black) may give you some degree of dominance on the page but unless it's done in good taste it can disrupt the image the store is trying to project. Discount and food stores often make use of reverse to draw attention to specific spots—usually prices—in otherwise busy ads. Flex-form is another option certain newspapers offer. This process al-

SMALL SPACE ADS present a challenge to copywriters: how to draw a reader's eye to your little spot on the page. *Courtesy 1740 House, Verbatim, L. L. Bean, Inc. and Preferred Hotels Association.*

lows an irregularly shaped ad, with newspaper stories set to match the contours of your ad. The increase in attention value of the unexpected shape heightens interest in your message. Flexform is not always available, but you should know enough to ask— just in case it serves your needs.

Newspaper color

It's becoming increasingly common for local newspapers to offer advertisers the opportunity to use a second color (in addition to black, of course) at an extra charge. If this color can be used for good dramatic effect—to spotlight a package, for instance— it may help the ad's impact. But beware: to use a second color for its own sake is often a waste of money.

Classified advertising

Still another way to gain better readability for your writing efforts is a display-classified ad in the classified section. This lets you gain more attention on the classified page because your ad looks so different from the others on that page. Your display-classified ad allows copy in large size and sometimes even artwork, which is enough to make you stand out amid the clutter of the classified ads surrounding you.

Display-classified ads are highly suitable for apartments, automobiles, homes or practically any item normally sold via classified ads, which includes just about everything! If it's a big classified section, such as on Sunday in many cities, your display-classified ad should run on the same page as the classified ads for the product or service you're advertising so you can be sure that the people reading your ad are interested in what you're selling.

Many advertisers have found it helpful on occasion to run some small classified ads to help supplement their usual display ads. Remember, readers of classified ads are usually looking for something and so are prescreened by the category of the items in the classified columns. Small, relatively inexpensive classified ads can help stretch an otherwise tight ad budget. Most newspapers have special classified ad deals for month-long advertisers who keep the same copy in the ad.

And if your item is seasonal, such as snow tires, you can get a jump on timing by leaving an ad at the newspaper with instructions to run it the night of the first big snowstorm. Presto! Great timing—better readership for your ad.

Weekly Newspapers

Don't overlook what weekly newspapers can do for your creative efforts. Consider the older, established ones that can verify their circulation figures. While weeklies have less circulation than the daily papers, their rates are lower, and perhaps they can give you concentrated circulation in an area more receptive to your message. Weekly newspapers usually have a longer life span around the house and are often read more thoroughly because of local-interest items.

Printed inserts

Before leaving newspapers, consider an advertiser's own printed circular inserted in a daily or weekly newspaper. It can be cheaper than mailing the circular directly to people's homes. Such inserts are usually in magazine format and in color. They can be printed elsewhere and shipped to the newspaper. Many Sunday magazine supplements and comic sections work in the same way.

Franchised operations usually make inserts available to the local stores, who merely arrange to have their own name and address imprinted on the insert. The insert is put in the newspaper and both are delivered at the same time. Some newspapers offer different insert service for different sections of the city, particularly if they have zoned circulation routes. This could be an efficient way for an advertiser to reach certain suburban towns or just the inner-city area.

An insert is a proven device often used by all the merchants in a given shopping center. It allows them to pool their dollars to create a single ad unit that is delivered just to their own trade area.

Newspapers excel at offering free creative services. They will normally be glad to help a local retailer get some artwork together, write the copy and even do the layout.

DIALING IN RADIO

In most cities local radio is the nearest competition with local newspapers for the bulk of retail advertising dollars. When buying radio, the problems for a media buyer are generally more complicated because usually there are many local stations from which to choose. Radio commercials are usually 10, 30 or 60 seconds long.

Each station lays claim to a particular type of listening audience. This claim can help an advertiser "match" his target audience with the station's listener profile. If you live in the local community you probably are familiar with the stations' type of listeners. If not, most stations have such listener research available, or it can be found in *Standard Rate & Data* for spot radio.

Some of the basic "types" of radio stations are categorized by their programming: middle of the road, hard rock, country and western, foreign language, religious, black, to name some of the most common. Naturally, each type of programming attracts a certain demographically identifiable listener. Realizing this, you should be able to write copy that more directly plugs into the listeners' interests. Here again, medium and message should work together.

The *time* your commercials are to be aired is important, too. The night owls listening at 2 A.M. are much different from the commuters driving to and from work in the morning and evening rush hours.

The program content of the shows that will be heard before and after your commercial, if it's to be aired during the station break, can be important. Program content attracts certain audiences, such as housewives, young adults, children, sports fans. The Bird Watcher program aired over one radio station surely attracts a very specific audience at 9:15 A.M. Selection of the time for your radio spot in relation to program content around it is as critical as getting in the proper section of a newspaper. Advertising investments in media can be maximized by careful placement within each medium because your message will get increased atttention by your best potential customers.

Radio is relatively inexpensive in most localities. In fact, it's the least expensive when the cost for just one spot is considered. Radio spots can help back up your message in the local newspaper by running them at the same time. However, be sure both your print ads and your radio commercials are saying the same thing. A radio station will be glad to help you add music or sound effects to your commercial, usually without charge.

It's also worth noting that a number of advertisers who use TV have discovered they can increase the effectiveness of their TV investment by playing only the audio (sound) portion of the TV commercial in less-expensive radio spots. The radio-listening audience automatically "replays" the video (picture) part in their minds. This assumes sufficient investment has been made to make the audience familiar with the original TV commercial.

THE TV PICTURE

Unlike radio, TV is usually a more costly local medium, but just like radio there is no "reference" or "tear-out" value. Viewers cannot go back to reread either your radio or TV commercial, nor can they easily comparison shop. Likewise, radio listeners or TV viewers cannot clip your cents-off coupon the way it's done in print media.

However, for a product or service that sells primarily by demonstration, TV is without equal. TV is also an outstanding medium to use to help build an image for a local service or store. It's often too expensive to consider using TV to reinforce or supplement print ads—although a growing number of department stores and discount chains are beginning to do so. Radio can do this job much less expensively at the local level.

The use of TV by national manufacturers or large chains is entirely different than for local, retail use. This is further discussed in Chapter 4. TV commercials are usually 30 seconds in length, with some of 10 seconds and fewer of 60 seconds.

Prime time on TV falls between 7 and 11 P.M. (the hours vary according to time zone and station). Spots in this time span generally cost more than other viewing hours because more people are watching their television sets at this time. However, possibly your particular target audience views TV during the less expensive time slots. Again, watch the program content (programming). It could be to an advertiser's advantage to be on the air during the morning hours even if the total viewers are fewer if the product or service is of primary interest to housewives or young mothers. Or during a big sports event if the product is aimed at men. Every effort is made to be on the screen when the audience is composed of your likeliest prospects./

/Sometimes there are more advertisers who want prime time spots than there are spots available. (Print media can simply add extra pages when needed; TV stations are not as lucky.) This makes it all the more difficult for a media buyer to put together his "package." Network shows reach the entire country./Local stations broadcast only as far as their signal area.

MAGAZINE OPPORTUNITIES

While the medium-size, local retailer rarely has an advertising budget or trade area that will justify using magazines, more opportunities are becoming available as more locally published magazines are appearing—and as technology enables major national magazines to break out hundreds of geographic and demographic audience segments, discussed later.

Thinking about magazines as belonging to "groups" helps the media buyer make the selection. There's the home and shelter group of magazines, the men's adventure group, the weekly news groups, the teen-age group, the handyman group, the automobile and hot rod group, the yacht and sailing group—the list goes on and on. Such groupings are easily seen in a copy of *Standard Rate & Data* for consumer magazines.

Cost, of course, is a big factor in magazine space purchases. A single, 4-color page in *Reader's Digest* costs nearly $100,000 for one issue, plus art and production costs—and sometimes sales tax! Unlike some of the media discussed, most magazines do not help the larger advertisers get their ads together; they pay commissions to advertising agencies who, in turn, create the ads for their clients. There are always exceptions, of course, particularly among smaller magazines. It's best for smaller advertisers to write to the magazines they're considering for whatever help they can get. Some do give valuable hints and tips for small, mail-order type advertising.

Regional editions

Most major magazines now offer regional editions or even editions for major metropolitan areas. The editorial content (news and features) does not usually vary, but the advertising pages can be different in different editions. You'll rarely notice the difference as a casual reader unless your eye glances down to study the page-numbering sequence. If you see numbers such as 8A, 8B, 8C or JAX/1 you're probably reading a specialized, regional edition.

Because less circulation is sometimes more attractive to advertisers, *Time* magazine, for one, offers special editions that reach college students, businessmen and several other demographically identifiable groups. It also offers geographically selected circulation areas, including zip-code breakouts. For example, rather than buying the complete national circulation of *Time* at its national rates, an advertiser can save money by just buying the Southeastern edition or just certain key cities, such as Atlanta, Miami or Tampa/St. Petersburg.

Such regional and demographic editions continue to proliferate, and more are yet to come. Before long, advertisers can expect to find a number of large-circulation magazines offering custom-tailored editions which, at least in theory, could exclusively reach a specific demographic group, within a specific occupational category, in a specific geographic area, with a specific editorial interest. The technology is ready to allow an advertiser to appear in, say, copies of a mass magazine sent only to stamp collectors with management-professional titles, with minimum $25,000 household income in neighborhoods in North Central counties. The key to this flexibility is computer-controlled binding.

Large department stores have found it profitable to place full-page ads in regional or city editions of magazines that circulate in areas where the store has many branch operations. By doing this the store can easily tie in to whatever fashions or new ideas are being featured in the editorial columns of the publication. Also, there surely is a definite boost for the store's image to be advertising in what the reader considers to be a nationwide, prestige magazine; little does the average reader realize (or care) that the store has only purchased a limited geographical circulation of the magazine. This valuable way to increase the impact

Give your kids The Button and watch them develop.

Instant photography is one activity your kids can enjoy without taking a lesson, trying out for a team or joining a club.

You can introduce them to it with The Button, Polaroid's new fun camera.

More than a diverting pastime, The Button is a tool that helps kids learn by doing.

Young photographers can experiment with distances, angles and composition and see the results immediately. Which altogether increases learning and retention.

The Button doesn't take hours of practice to master. You just aim and shoot. And the camera delivers color pictures as fast as kids want answers: in seconds. For their efforts, aspiring artists are

rewarded not only with a beautiful picture, but with a sense of accomplishment.

Besides nurturing creative instincts, The Button develops social ones. It encourages kids to share. And even helps give them a better understanding of themselves and their friends.

What's more, for all the enrichment it provides, the camera is inexpensive.

There is, however, one more good reason to give your kids The Button. If you're on your best behavior, they just might agree to let you borrow it.

The Button from Polaroid.
The instant camera that develops kids.

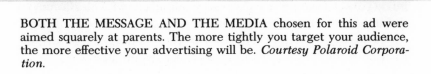

BOTH THE MESSAGE AND THE MEDIA chosen for this ad were aimed squarely at parents. The more tightly you target your audience, the more effective your advertising will be. *Courtesy Polaroid Corporation.*

of your message merely through the use of peculiarities of a medium should be more closely monitored by copywriters.

Such a concept is also valuable for manufacturers who are test marketing a product and/or have limited distribution in a specific geographical area. Or for nonprofit organizations (including universities) who realize the majority of their enrollment comes from a definite geographical area.

Preferred positions

Just like newspapers, magazines have preferred positions that have proven to boost readership of advertising. Invariably, these positions are reserved in advance and priced at premium rates. The back cover is one such spot, for obvious reasons. So is the inside of the front cover (called the "second cover") and the inside of the back cover (known as the "third cover").

A "gatefold" is another idea that costs extra. Such a device is commonly incorporated into the front cover of a magazine which unfolds outward to give the advertiser a dramatic double-size display area inside the cover. Double gatefolds are sometimes used in conjunction with the center spread in magazines, too. Quarter or third page gatefolds ("flaps") are also made available by certain magazines. All these options are expensive. You should know that many advertisers think the added impact is worth it.

Other less costly preferred positions include near the letters-to-the-editor section, near the table of contents or near a well-read feature. Some magazines may charge for these locations; others will be glad to put your message there if they know that's what you want. Still other advertisers insist on being toward the front of the book (magazine), where the articles begin, rather than in the back with all the helter-skelter continuations. Many magazines have articles starting throughout the publication, which helps solve this problem.

The right-hand page versus the left-hand page, discussed earlier in newspaper ad placement, comes up again in magazines. There is conflicting feeling among media buyers. However, you might study your own magazine reading habits. Do you cover the left-hand page when holding the magazine? Does your eye travel first to the right-hand page? But then again, don't you read both the left- and right-hand pages eventually?

Center spreads in magazines are attractive, but expensive. This is where the magazine naturally opens at the middle and allows you to have your message printed continuously across the two pages without interruption by a "gutter" (blank space in the middle). The only pitfall here for a copywriter is: be careful where the binding staples hit your ad. A pen company unfortunately used a beautiful piece of artwork only to have the magazine's binding staples intrude right over the pen just behind the tip of the point.

Another danger that could affect the impact of your carefully worded and designed ad is the use of two facing pages in a magazine that are not the center spread. Here the headline or artwork can be badly misaligned between one page and the next. A cruise line once ran a glamorous picture of one of its ships across such a spread, only to have the ship look as if it had been sliced in half and was sinking! When this happens, it's certainly not your fault as the copywriter, but it surely may diminish the credibility of your message and the overall impact you wanted your copy to achieve.

Unusual positions

Some positions that will earn more attention for your message when using smaller space are available in many magazines. Your ad in an "island" puts reading material around it on all four sides and usually lets your advertising message dominate the entire page without paying for a full page. Also, some magazines offer opposite-corner positions—called "checkerboards." In this layout, your ad appears in the top left-hand corner of the page and your other ad in the lower right-hand corner of the opposite page. Your message dominates the pages without paying the cost of a full page. The size of each ad is about ¼ page. Keep these opportunities in mind as you plan your ad.

There are still other ways to maximize the readership of your ad in magazines even if your firm or client has a small budget. As mentioned for newspapers, a horizontal half page across the entire bottom or top may be available. Flexform is available in some magazines, too, giving your message extra attention.

Magazines normally offer better color reproduction than most newspapers because they're printed on better stock (paper) on

Now you can kill wasps and hornets in their nests from...

over." He saw Ty cast an anxious look toward Maggie's open door. "I won't hurt her," Chase added. "I won't go near her tonight, so you can rest easy."

Ty accepted his father's word and retraced the steps to his bedroom while Chase continued slowly to his own.

Dawn came in changing sheets of color. As the sun peered over a hill at the new day, Chase shaved and dressed. Ty was walking down the hall when Chase left his room. They nodded a good morning and continued toward the staircase. As they passed Maggie's room, where the broken door sagged open, Ty glanced inside.

"Mom isn't up." He gave a questioning look to Chase. Chase's stride didn't falter as he passed the door, briefly glimpsing black hair against a white pillow. "Let her sleep."

After breakfast Ty left the house to do his morning chores, and Chase went out to check the previous day's work and make any last-minute adjustments in the day's schedule for the crews. An hour later he returned to the ranch house. It was silent, nothing and no one stirring. He climbed the stairs to Maggie's room.

Crossing the threshold that he had not stepped past the night before, he walked to the bed to wake her. Chase looked at her sleeping form, the slim, white shoulders bare except for the narrow straps of her night gown. He touched her shoulder, and she sat up suddenly. Confusion, shock, anger, and sleep were all mixed in her expression as she pushed the weight of her rumpled hair from her face.

"It's time to get up," he said, his gaze drifting to the front of her nightgown.

She turned her head to see the morning sun shining in the window, and she hurriedly swung her feet out of the bed. "Why didn't you wake me earlier?"

"There's no need to rush. Ty and I have already had breakfast." Chase was totally unnerved by the

and held her breath. She didn't want him near her. She didn't want to smell another woman's perfume on his skin—every part of her rebelled at the thought.

There was no thought in his mind beyond catching her and putting down this insurrection in his home. He grabbed the doorknob, but it wouldn't yield to the pressure of his hand. His fist pounded on the solid door. "Maggie! Open up!" The command was a low roar.

"Go away!"

"You unlock this door, or I swear I'll break it in!" he warned and rattled the knob again.

This time there was no reply, only silence from within. Once he'd made his intention clear, he couldn't back down. Stepping back, he kicked at the center of the thick oak door near the lock. It shook and held. With a second kick, Chase heard the faint splintering of wood. Putting all his force behind the blow, he kicked at the door again and felt the sickening give of the wood. When his boot hit the same weakened area again, there was a ripping sound as the metal lock was torn out of the frame and the door whipped open.

Breathing heavily from the exertion, he saw Maggie standing well back from the door holding on to the bedpost that was behind her back. A wariness blazed from her. "Don't you come near me," she warned. "You have no right in this room unless I invite you. And I don't want you to touch me!"

Her icy rejection made Chase retaliate in kind. "What makes you think I would be interested?" He had the satisfaction of seeing her wince at his contemptuous reply.

Turning on his heel, he started toward his own room and stopped when he saw Ty staring at him from the end of the hall. The bewildered look of alarm in his son's face washed away his rage. Tiredness swept through him, slumping his shoulders.

"Go to bed, son," he said in a weary voice. "It's all

247

...12 ft. away!

Raid Wasp & Hornet Killer has a long-distance spray-nozzle to keep you at a good distance. You spray it directly on the nest. It kills on contact and saturates the nest to kill late-coming or returning insects. Use it once and the job is done.

Raid

Johnson wax

© 1978 S. C. Johnson & Son, Inc.

FULL-PAGE IMPACT comes from two quarter-page ads working in tandem in this highly effective "checkerboard" arrangement. *Courtesy S. C. Johnson & Son, Inc.*

which a finer screen (reproduction method) can be used. Other than the cost of space in magazines, another problem for an advertiser (and for you as a copywriter) is the long lead time required before publication of your ad. A monthly magazine can easily have a deadline six to eight weeks in advance of actual publication. And the reality of only 12 issues a year for a monthly can pose the problem of insufficient frequency for proper message exposure. Of course, weekly magazines require less production lead time.

The press of business

For every business, trade or profession, there is a magazine or newspaper. These publications are known, not surprisingly, as trade, business or professional publications. They represent a preselected target for your message based on reader interest of the specialized editorial content.

Not to be confused with newsstand "consumer" publications, these publications usually never enter the home but are delivered to a place of business. They are truly part of the vast communication iceberg that's rarely seen by the consumer in the street. Of course, there are a few notable exceptions, including *Women's Wear Daily* and *The Wall Street Journal,* that are available at some newsstands in larger cities.

Standard Rate & Data for business publications is a reference volume that completely categorizes these publications, which offer an excellent way for your message to reach directly interested doctors, lawyers, grocery buyers, electronics manufacturers, teachers, sportswear buyers—you name it. There was even a magazine for the funeral trade named *Casket & Sunnyside* that's now more discreetly called *C&S.*

SALES DISPLAYS (POINT-OF-PURCHASE)

Where are they going to put it? The copywriter who is given the task of helping create an interesting POP display should carefully consider where the retailer might have space for it. And is the manufacturer willing to pay to get the space (either in cash or free goods)? He doesn't always have to, but he should be prepared. Most POP displays are probably thrown out unused or stashed in a back room. Sad but true.

There are so many variations of POP displays that only your own creativity can limit the types of designs, working with an artist, of course. However, while counter space is almost impossible to get in the typical retail store, remember the ceiling, walls and floor.

An interesting mobile or other hanging-type display is not normally as costly as one constructed to put on the floor. "Shelf-talkers" attached to supermarket shelves or in the frozen food cabinets don't take that much space either and are relatively inexpensive to produce. And they're really at the right spot at the moment of buying decision! A freestanding "island" display is another location that gets good attention.

However, if you're going to help design a POP display by writing the copy that's to go on it, remember that it will most likely be seen from more than one angle—maybe from all four sides. You may get more involved in this display project than you ever anticipated. If you do, beware of displays that are self-contained (with merchandise inside). Consider the weight and balance factor. Will it still spin or even stand up when only half full of hair brushes? When totally full? When there's only one brush left? If you're working with a designer-manufacturer, be sure he makes one working sample before you start up the approval steps. Fill it up. Will it really work? Indeed, a copywriter gets involved in some very eventful projects!

OUTDOOR ADVERTISING

Outdoor advertising is generally identified as the billboards you see along busy streets and highways. Legislation has restricted the use of billboards along the U.S. Interstate system, but there are still enough high-traffic locations remaining to make this a sound medium. Outdoor advertising generally supports an ongoing campaign in other media. Billboards declaring "This is Marlboro Country" are only meaningful because of the other consistent efforts by Marlboro over the years.

A medium of this nature can be very valuable in reaching your target on the move: while a person travels to shop or commutes to work. Due to the nature of the space available, your message must be very short and dynamic. Food items, travel items, impulse items, automobiles and their accessories all lend themselves very well to outdoor billboards and other sign treatment. So do such services as motels, restaurants and tourist attractions. One radio station advertised on an outdoor billboard located on a heavily used commuter bridge: "We spent today with your wife. Welcome home."

Outdoor locations should be selected carefully and the media buyer should personally "ride the showing" to check each location before renting it. He should be sure the sign is at a good angle to the traffic flow; a right angle usually assures excellent viewing; signs parallel to the roadway should be avoided. He should try to rent signs that have some relationship to the audience that's traveling a path of interest to his product or service. Airlines, for example, might consider main arteries leading to the airport for passengers who have yet to buy their tickets.

Other factors to consider when using this medium include illumination, size, use of cut-out art for silhouettes, flip-flop boards (multi messages that change on the same board, also known as multiple vision) and animated art, such as a spinning bicycle wheel.

Locations are rented in "showings." If an advertiser rents a "100 showing," it means he has rented enough outdoor locations to saturate that geographical area. Of course, he can rent fewer locations too. Outdoor boards are normally rented on a 30-day basis.

Outdoor advertising can achieve impressive results. The Institute of Outdoor Advertising dramatized this recently by posting the name and photograph of the then-current Miss America, wearing her crown, on 10,000 billboards across the country. That's right, just her name and picture. The experiment was intended to prove how the outdoor medium could get a message to the public. Before the test, a random sample showed that only 1.6 percent of the American public knew her name. After two months, the same question was asked and this time the awareness shot up to 16.3 percent—a 900 percent increase! What more can be said—except, keep outdoor advertising in mind as you write your advertising.

We live up to

OUTDOOR BILLBOARDS get a driver's attention for a very few seconds. The message must be briefly stated in order to be quickly grasped. Such advertising often relies, as here, on strong visual support. *Courtesy Sunkist Growers, Inc.*

DIRECT MAIL

Chances are your name is on a number of mailing lists right now. Think about what has been in your mailbox lately. Offers from book clubs? Mail order houses? Newly minted coin collections? Your name is on a list that each of these companies purchased for the purpose of aiming its offers at a definite type of prospect. What list? Maybe your magazine subscription. Or credit card. Or the alumni directory from your school or college. A firm that wants to reach a particular type of person tries to buy a list that comes closest to this profile. As you can imagine, there's a fairly brisk business in buying and selling lists like this!

our word.

Direct mail represents a big chunk of ad dollars. (For more on the entire "direct response" field, see page 121). And it's growing larger every year, as life-styles change and new habits are acquired. People are learning how convenient it is to shop at home (something Sears, Roebuck and Company discovered generations ago!), avoiding crowds, saving time—and now saving on expensive gasoline! No matter what area of advertising you're in, you'll probably be asked to write direct mail copy from time to time.

Direct mail differs from other forms of advertising in two important respects. First of all, you don't have to go to great lengths to attract the reader's attention. If the person opens the mail, your message gets read automatically—at least the headline. If the person doesn't open the mail, then you could stand on your head in striped pajamas for all the good it would do. Second, if the mailing list has been chosen carefully, the reader is a genuine candidate to heed what you're saying. This means you've got the attention of a real, live prospect. What do you say to clinch the sale?

A key point to bear in mind is that what you say at this point is more important than how you say it. Remember, this is a hot lead. Plain talk with a very clear promise will do the trick. Also, any way that you can involve the reader will lift the level of response appreciably. A classic example: the ad that says "If you can draw me, you have the talent we're looking for." Over the years, how many people have played this little game and enrolled at the art school because the advertising got them involved?

However, direct mail programs are not cheap. (Consider postage costs alone!) They have to be monitored carefully. Follow-up has to be consistent.

Many authorities in direct mail feel a 3% return is good. That means that if you mail 1,000, look for possibly 30 replies. That's all—and that's good! The moral of this exercise in mathematics is, first, in direct mail, mail a lot of it, and, second, use a good, current, reliable mailing list. Such a list should represent your best potential customers and be free of "deadwood." It should not have wrong addresses, people who have died or moved or people who are no longer your best potential customers.

Companies that compile and sell such lists can be found in the Yellow Pages in any major city. They'll make a list available for almost any category you want to reach, from helicopter pilots to English teachers. Some creative considerations involved in direct mail are discussed in Chapter 7.

TRANSIT ADVERTISING

Transit advertising appears on the inside and outside of public transportation vehicles—buses, subways, commuter railroad cars. The outside ads are really moving billboards and should be designed as such. Very simple. Strong graphics. Few words. The

"Cruise Allowance Check"

Are your vacation dates fixed?

Do you require an advance reservation (more than five days) to pack and say "Goodbye" to friends and neighbors? Holland America Cruises saves you up to $300 per couple when you vacation on a 7-day cruise to Bermuda.

Here is all you have to do ... Take the above "Cruise Allowance Check" to your local Travel Agent who will help you select a departure date and cabin in our available outside twin accommodations. Prices start from $1020. per person. A 25% deposit is required when you make a reservation. The balance is payable no later than eight (8) weeks prior to cruise departure. Full payment is required at the time of booking if reservations are made within eight (8) weeks. See the terms & conditions for this program on page 6.

"PERSONALIZED" DIRECT MAIL can be highly effective, especially when coupled, as it is here, with a valuable "check" if the offer is accepted. *Courtesy Holland America Cruises.*

category of product or service can be almost anything because the audience will be people outside the vehicle, either pedestrians or drivers of automobiles.

The advertising inside public vehicles—usually called "car cards" or "end cards," depending on the shape of the ad and where it's placed in the vehicle—is different. As you might expect, there's more time for a passenger to read your ad so you can make use of more copy than is advisable for outside ads. The audience composition is different, too. There are many more youngsters and elderly, for one thing. It's also generally a lower socioeconomic group so it's not the prime audience for high-ticket products or high-fashion retail establishments. However, the demographic composition of commuter rail and bus lines in large metropolitan areas, such as New York or Chicago, often compares favorably to, say, *Time* magazine, and your advertising appeals can be adjusted accordingly.

ADVERTISING SPECIALTIES

Everything from a kite in the sky to a key ring in your pocket can be devised to carry your advertising message. Specialty items have come a long way since the days of giveaway calendars with the advertiser's name, address and phone number. (Although this is still a popular item!) Now, of course, the selection of such items is endless. You might even have an imprinted pen in your pocket right now, or a bumper sticker for a tourist attraction decorating your car. The best suggestion when using this advertising medium is to pick an item that relates to the business or product so it becomes a timely reminder to the target audience. Also, the item should be something that could possibly be seen by more than just the person it's given to. A bicycle shop, for example, might select an imprinted handlebar decoration.

DIRECTORIES

In a highly mobile community, such as one near a government installation, resort or university, the Yellow Pages and other helpful directories are particularly worth serious consideration. Tenants or homeowners can move so quickly that the newcomers need a speedy reference source for dozens of products and services, such as plumbers, appliances, churches, motels and so on. *Thomas Register* serves the same purpose in the industrial world. Most public libraries have a copy of it for your inspection.

OTHER MEDIA

You may create advertisements on film to show in theaters. Or you may design slide presentations for sales representatives to show to dealers. Individual cassettes, phonograph records or a sign pulled across the sky over a crowded football stadium may be writing assignments that cross your desk in the future, too. The medium to be used for each job is an important consideration when planning what to say and how to say it. Then, too, it should be very obvious by now that what the media buyer does can easily affect the effectiveness of your work.

Applying
psychology

4

You've probably heard the terms "hard sell" and "soft sell" and might figure that all advertising had to fall into one category or the other. That notion is more convenient than it is accurate. Start thinking of "smart sell," because that's the secret of the very best ads. "Smart sell" takes careful planning, but is much more likely to get the results you're after.

Do not begin by sitting down and starting to write. That comes later—much later. If you start right out by putting words on paper, without taking certain preliminary steps, you'll end up talking to yourself, hearing only what *you* want to hear.

This means that when you get an assignment, you should resist the temptation to grab a pencil or rush to the typewriter and start doing your thing. What would come out of this haste? A statement of facts (benefits) that you know the product possesses or is capable of delivering. It might never occur to you that what you think is all-important is ho-hum to those people you're trying to influence.

For example, you have a new shampoo to launch and you know its formulation is less harsh on hair than the other shampoos that line the shelves. True enough. That's what the people in the laboratory say—and can prove. That's what the product manager is enthusiastic about. But you shouldn't hurry back to your desk and write that this new shampoo is "less harsh" or "more gentle" in unadorned glory of the facts. Not at all. First, pry from the manufacturer every fact about the product you can— even those some may think are unimportant. Then make sure you have a carefully defined target audience. Finally, dig, dig, dig for a benefit based on the facts that would stimulate this specific audience about this specific product.

The end result might be something such as "Now you can wash your hair every night without worry." You'll notice it says "less harsh" in terms that relate clearly to a consumer need. That's because you've discovered the audience for this product doesn't want a "less harsh" shampoo. They don't perceive their problem in those terms. They have a fear that frequent washing will damage their hair structure. They want a product that will erase this fear. Our "less harsh" shampoo does this, but until its benefit is stated in terms that are meaningful to the audience, the message will probably go unheard and—more important—the product will never find its way onto a shopping list.

TEACH, DON'T TELL

So the way to begin is to keep a tight check on yourself. Don't race from the starting gate. Slow down. The biggest mistake you can make is telling people what *you* think they should know— for their own good. The motive behind this kind of thinking might be exemplary. But nobody wants to be told what's good for him or her by a perfect stranger demonstrating what might seem to be superior intelligence. Remember you're in possession of certain facts, just as your audience is aware of certain needs. The trick is to match things up so everybody's happy. It's easier said than done.

CHOOSE YOUR TARGET

Who is your target? Maybe you'd like to think that it's everyone under the sun, but don't count on it. Even such broad-appeal

THINK OF THIS AS THE WINDOW OFFICE YOU ALWAYS WANTED.

Climbing the corporate ladder, Amtrak's a great way to get there.

Uninterrupted travel time to use productively. A wide, plush seat. Lots of room to lean back and stretch out. Plus a cafe car for refreshments and relaxation.

If you're already there, join the club—our premium-service club cars on many departures, with service right at your seat.

Before your next business trip, call your travel agent or Amtrak. It makes good business sense.

Amtrak ➤ AMERICA'S GETTING INTO TRAINING

BOTH THE HEADLINE AND PICTURE present the advantages of rail travel in an original way that should trigger the desired response among its business-executive target group. *Courtesy Amtrak.*

products as soaps and soft drinks don't try to address everyone. Soap ads are aimed at shoppers who make purchase decisions (mostly women) while soft drinks zero in on the thirsty younger generation (although this will clearly change as the age curve skews higher). If these two very general categories of consumer goods set their sights so sharply, should your product do less? This is where a little research comes in very handy.

In an advertising agency, you will probably be buried by an avalanche of data from a variety of different sources. No effort will be spared to define the target group in terms of age, sex, income level, ethnic group and other relevant characteristics that will affect the way the appeal is framed. This kind of thorough demographic breakdown is reassuring but not always foolproof.

If you're on the advertising staff of a manufacturer, it's also quite likely you'll be able to tap ample data sources to pinpoint your target. There's no way to stress how important this is. You almost have to have a mental picture of the face, the home and the bankbook of the person you're talking to. Because that's exactly what you're doing: talking to one person, face to face, one to one. If you can't visualize who that person is and what he or she looks like, you're going to have trouble knowing what words to say and what tone to use.

Outside an advertising agency or a manufacturing company, chances are you're going to be left largely to your own resources. But that can often be enough. All it takes is a willingness to step back from your own preconceived ideas about the product you know so well. Ask yourself, who can reasonably expect to be a prospect? Men? Women? Teenagers? (Teens have plenty of money to spend these days, in case you haven't noticed.)

Don't always accept the easy answer. At one time all airline advertising was directed at men until it was learned through various studies that women played a decisive role in final travel decisions. Another example is that although almost half the deodorant users in the country are men, research showed that over 80 percent of the purchases were made by women. In other words, to sell deodorants to men, you have to appeal to women. Maybe the *Ladies Home Journal* had it right a few years back when its rallying cry was "Never underestimate the power of a woman."

DO YOUR OWN RESEARCH

What makes people make a choice? You'll never understand the reasons unless you get out of the office and into the shopping places. Watch people shop. See who takes the product off the shelf. Talk to her, or him. Ask why that particular product was selected when there were probably dozens of other choices available. But don't always accept "low price" as an answer. People always want to give the impression that they're smart shoppers (don't you?) so they often supply an answer that reflects this. Of course, you can't do too much probing in an informal situation like this, but with a little experience you'll be able to tell when a person really means "low price *in a brand I've learned to trust.*"

If you have an idea maybe you might want to try it out here. Ask that shopper, "Suppose I told you that this brand of paper hankie won't shred when you use it—would you buy it?" Don't be surprised at the answer. She might say, "That's great." Or she might shrug, "So what?" because she has no dissatisfaction with the brand she now uses. The whole point of this exercise is to check whether an idea that sounds promising in the office has much appeal at the point of sale.

As said before, you're trying to match the benefit in the product with the perceived needs of the prospects. And it's not always what you think! So any research you can devise will go a long way toward determining the right way to trigger the response you want.

And don't be disturbed by the fact that your rather casual research doesn't have all the "scientific" hallmarks of a Gallup poll. There's really no such thing as a sure thing in the world of research. Sophisticated questionnaires may look impressive and lengthy computer printouts might seem awesomely authoritative, but even all this never quite provides the final answer. The results are no more than signposts. It always winds up with people—like you—making the final decisions long after the computer has exhausted its resources. Also see Chapter 11, Copy Research.

COMMON SENSE

You have what the computer lacks—common sense. The chances are that you have more than you think.

• It takes common sense to view your product through the eyes of the prospect rather than with your own myopic vision.

• It takes common sense to understand that everyone won't be as taken with your product as you are.

• It takes common sense to realize that what you think is "gee whiz" about your product might cause a polite yawn when seen by a potential customer.

• It takes common sense to listen to other viewpoints, to appreciate that different people have different likes and dislikes, to accept the fact that your own personal feelings don't necessarily represent those of the people you're trying to persuade.

If you've ever sat in a room and listened to two people discuss a product, you know what happens. One will swear by a certain brand—it could be beer or paper towels or anything. He or she might describe the trial and error process that led to the choice. The other frequently has another brand preference and will argue that he or she has tried the others and found another to be superior. Both are right, of course; different people want different things in a product and perceive that they get them in the brand they finally choose.

In the case of these two people, it's perfectly all right for them to feel the way they do and to cling stubbornly to their positions. It's something called brand loyalty, and no branded product can survive long without it. But unlike these two people, the professional advertising person can't afford that kind of luxury. The moment you get so close to the product that you cannot understand how others can continue to be blind to its obvious virtues—that's when trouble begins. You must learn to subordinate your ego to your prospect's ego for the purpose of making a sale. And the customer is always right.

TWO RULES TO REMEMBER

1. Know Thy Product. This should be obvious. Know it inside and out. What goes into it. How it works. What it has that competitive products don't have. (And what the competition has that yours lacks!) You'll probably gather a thousand times more information than you'll ever use in an ad. But you'll also be prepared to recognize an opportunity when it presents itself because you will have the facts.

A number of years ago a beer company's advertising agency recommended a campaign based on the fact that the company steam-cleaned its bottles (remember, these were deposit bottles) before refilling them with beer. "But everyone does that," protested the beer people. "Yes, but who knows that except people in the beer business?" answered the agency. The upshot was that the advertising ran and turned out to be very successful. The point is, if the copywriter didn't know the previously obscure fact about the steam-cleaning, he wouldn't have been able to capitalize on it when he got all his other data assembled. *Know Thy Product.*

2. *Know Thy Prospects.* They may not be who you think they are. Find them. Study them. Listen to them. Try to put yourself in their shoes: see things through their eyes. Maybe they couldn't care less about a feature that sends you sky high. That doesn't make them wrong and you right. You live and breathe your product; they don't. They have other things on their minds besides what you're trying to sell them. They have bills to pay, houses to clean, children to educate. Important as your product is to you, it's probably a very minor concern to them. Don't fight this, accept it. You've simply got to break through this boredom barrier to make a sale. It won't be easy but unless you understand the nature of the people you're trying to reach, you don't stand a chance. *Know Thy Prospects.*

BENEFIT SELECTION

Effective advertising consists of making the right promise to the right audience. Simple, right? All you have to do is find the most desired benefit that your product is capable of delivering and then zero in on those who are most likely to gain the greatest advantage from this benefit.

Most production engineers and manufacturers think about features: the mechanical parts that make things work. Salesmen and copywriters think about features, too, but they also think strongly in terms of benefits: what can the feature do for somebody? Normally when benefits are meaningful to your target audience and are clearly stated in your headline and/or illustration, interest in your ad increases.

Another way to describe the difference between features and benefits is that features are built into the product when it comes off the assembly line. The copywriter can't do anything about the engineering of the product—there it is. But the feature usually leads to a benefit and that's where the copywriter must start to crank up his creative thinking.

Advertising copy that is loaded only with product features usually is weak "so what" copy. Product benefits are what make the difference. Your copy should mention the feature and then immediately give the benefit in terms meaningful to your target audience.

Hopefully, the feature will be unique: a thinner cigarette, a new flavor of yogurt, a hair spray that's not an aerosol. But more often than not, you will be dealing with a "parity" product, one that's essentially identical with competitive products in the category. There will be no real difference until you "create" one— that is, find a benefit that makes a customer prefer your brand over all those others on the shelf at the moment of decision.

After that, you have to be sure that this advertising is placed before the audience that's most likely to be affected by the appeal you're making. You wouldn't advertise a new female cosmetic in *Popular Mechanics* nor would you buy space in *Good Housekeeping* to announce a new computer system. These are obvious examples, of course. It's not always this cut and dried. Just remember this: if the benefit doesn't click with the target audience, you laid an egg. Altogether too much advertising ignores this simple fact, for one reason or another, and ends up talking to itself. A very expensive conversation!

HELP SOLVE PROBLEMS

"There are two kinds of advertising," a wise ad man once said, " 'me' advertising and 'you' advertising." "Me" advertising simply brags about how good the product is; "you" advertising conveys a sense of caring for the reader's real needs, describing how the product can be of help, solve some problem or satisfy the reader in some way. Sometimes this even calls for reminding the reader there is this need and then convincing him or her that your product is the answer!

If advertising doesn't persuade somebody to consider buying the product—either immediately or at some future time—then it has failed and somebody's money has been wasted. Haven't we all heard a guest at a party recall a "great" ad or television commercial, often repeating whatever catchphrase was used, and then fail to remember whether the product was made by Westinghouse or General Electric? The advertising graveyard is littered with campaigns that caught the public fancy but failed to boost the sales curve. If you keep people too busy laughing or remembering your clever lines, they apparently may forget who you are.

Advertising is not entertainment. It's business. Its first priority is selling something. This even goes for so-called corporate advertising, in which a company tries to win "influence leaders" to its point of view or summon interest in its stock. Those who sponsor such advertising clearly consider its commercial necessity, or else it would never appear.

SMILES MEAN SALES

Still, advertising can be amusing. It doesn't have to be dull. It was one of the first singing commercials, after all, that put Pepsi-Cola on the map many years ago. But what a whale of a lot of hard sell was packed in the famous four-line jingle that had all America singing:

Pepsi-Cola hits the spot   (You'll like the taste.)
Twelve full ounces, that's a lot.   (You'll like the size.)
Twice as much for a nickel, too.   (You'll like the price.)
Pepsi-Cola is the drink for you.   (You'll like feeling
                     smart for knowing all
                     this.)

© 1940 Pepsi-Cola Company. Reprinted with permission of PepsiCo Inc.

Pepsi-Cola never lost sight of its primary mission, which was to make consumers plunk down a nickel for a Pepsi instead of another drink. This ditty gave listeners four good reasons to make this decision in Pepsi-Cola's favor—and make them smile while doing it. But the smile never got in the way of the sale.

So your goal is to unearth whatever it is your product offers that matches up with some perceived need of the target group that you have determined is the best market for your product. What can your product do faster or easier or cheaper or more reliably than the other products from which your audience will make a choice?

UNIQUE SELLING PROPOSITION

A product's benefit claim has different names in different places. Among other names, you'll hear it called a "Position" or a "Target Response Statement." Here we will call it a Unique Selling Proposition (USP). Determining it is an essential first step in preparing any advertising.

What makes your product different—and presumably better—than all those other products it's competing with? If you were on the other side of the fence—the buyer rather than the seller—what would you be looking for in this type of product or service? And face it, very few people leaf through the pages of a newspaper or magazine looking for new ways to spend money. At best, they are in the market for a certain type of product and generally on the lookout for the one that appears to best meet their needs. More than likely, however, your reader will be much more casual about it, feeling no particular desire for this particular product at this particular time. (But because this might change in the future, an advertiser always strives to create and then maintain a favorable image in a customer's memory bank.)

In any event, you should present a good, strong reason to buy. If your potential prospects aren't given a strong reason to make a decision in your favor, they won't. It's that simple. All effective advertising starts right here. Often, but not necessarily, this springs from some unique attribute possessed by your product.

USPs for national ads

The psychological impression sought for products appearing in national media is quite different from the impression sought

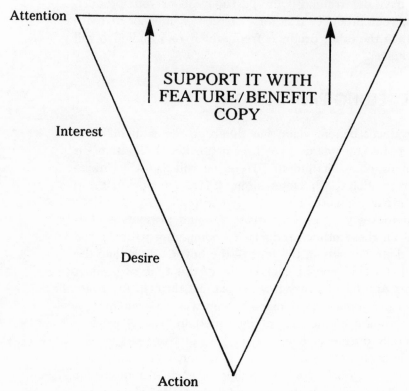

UNIQUE SELLING PROPOSITION*

Attention

SUPPORT IT WITH
FEATURE/BENEFIT
COPY

Interest

Desire

Action

Give your audience a strong <u>reason to buy</u> . . . fast!

*what your competition cannot say . . .
or is not saying at the present time

Kodak brings the instant closer.

Take pictures at normal distance.

Or close up.

Introducing the Kodak Colorburst 350.
The only instant camera with a built-in close-up lens.

Our exclusive built-in close-up lens and our built-in electronic flash let you take beautiful instant color pictures from as close as two feet away–in any light. Color pictures that are sharp, rich, vivid. And, best of all, also built in are 100 years of Kodak experience. The Colorburst 350 is the perfect instant camera for you and the perfect gift.

Kodak brings the instant to life!

© Eastman Kodak Company, 1981

NATIONAL ADVERTISING is largely found in magazines and network television and endeavors to precondition prospects by presenting a strong "reason why" story. The expected response is: "That's very nice. I should look into it next time I'm in a camera store." *Courtesy Eastman Kodak Company.*

Fun money

Have fun with a $10 rebate from Kodak on the new Kodak Colorburst 350 or the 250 instant camera.

A Kodak instant camera makes every occasion more fun because the pictures develop before everyone's eyes. And now you can get a $10 rebate on these fun-filled cameras.

Choose the Kodak Colorburst 250 instant camera with the handy built-in flash. Or get closer with the Kodak Colorburst 350 instant camera. It's the only instant camera with both a built-in close-up lens and a built-in flash. Plus, both cameras use Kodak instant color film for sharp, vivid color pictures. Just follow the instructions on this coupon to get in on the fun. And the ten dollars.

© Eastman Kodak Company, 1981

TAKE THE MONEY FOR FUN.

Please send me a $10 rebate on my purchase of:
☐ a Kodak Colorburst 250 instant camera or outfit.
☐ a Kodak Colorburst 350 instant camera.

1. Complete the address portion of this certificate.
2. Enclose the clip-off number tab from inside the box flap. (For Kodak Colorburst 250 outfits only, enclose the Universal Product Code cut from the back of the camera carton.)
3. Enclose dated sales receipt. Camera must be purchased between April 1, 1981, and August 31, 1981.

This request must be postmarked no later than September 30, 1981. Participation limited to one rebate per customer. All three items must be submitted before a rebate payment can be made. Send coupon and proofs of purchase to:
Take the Money for Fun Rebate, P.O. Box NB-073, El Paso, Texas 79977

Name _____
(Please print)
Address _____
City _____ State _____ Zip _____
Dealer Name: _____
City _____ State _____
(Please allow 6-8 weeks for delivery.)

KODAK BRINGS THE INSTANT TO LIFE.

LOCAL PRINT ADVERTISING most often appears in newspapers and has a very immediate goal. It has an urgent tone, demands action *now*, and is often price-oriented. *Courtesy Eastman Kodak Company.*

when the same products appear in local media. The reason? Think about the way you read the ads in *Time* magazine versus the way you read the ads in your hometown newspaper. To see this difference vividly, just compare a magazine ad for Sears, RCA, or Ford with an ad for the same product that appears in the local press. The first is more "image" oriented while the second is often "price" oriented.

National consumer advertising usually has as its goal preconditioning the target audience to look for and accept your product when it's offered locally in the community. Network television is a key medium for this kind of advertising. So are most magazines, inasmuch as their distribution (unlike newspapers) extends beyond the market area of any retail establishment. This advertising must convince the target to assign a high priority to your product whether purchase is imminent (in the case of a person coughing from a cold who is persuaded to try the cough suppressant shown on the screen) or in the case of a family planning to buy a new car sometime this year.

Bear in mind, too, that the psychological set of your audience varies in different media and this will also affect the way you approach your creative presentation. The time factor is one such consideration. Television is fleeting, so your message must be communicated clearly, memorably, dramatically—and quickly. Your audience can't go back to reread the copy. When it's over, it's gone for good. On the other hand, many magazines get up to four hours of reading time. There's an opportunity to develop a thought and pursue it to conclusion. This does not mean that magazine ads can be any less dramatic or attention-getting. But studies show that magazine readers are more apt to give good ads a reading and certainly readers have a chance to dwell on your copy points far longer than when watching television. From this you can see that the psychological set of your audience will differ by medium; it's up to you to make these differences work to your advantage.

The goal here is to familiarize an audience with the virtues of a product so that it will accept the product when reminded of it by local advertising or when confronted by it at the point of sale. The following list might help you identify the unique features of your product that can become the basis for your advertising:

• *Physical, Tangible Product Attributes*

Form—gel toothpaste
Color—blue soap pads
Fragrance—lime shaving cream
Flavor—old-fashioned root beer

• *Advantages Resulting from Manufacture*

Packaging—individually wrapped sleeves of crackers in box
Size—miniature salt containers
Economy—more squares of bath tissue per roll
New process—freeze-dried coffee

• *Advantages Related to Marketing Strategy*

Exclusiveness—the only early morning flight from Pittsburgh to Kalamazoo
Convenience—half-size cans of soup for one-person households
Warranty—3-year protection plan for car owners
Price—a great gift idea for under $100

You get the idea. Now you know what to look for. Sometimes it's obscure and has to be found. At other times it's so obvious it goes without notice. Finding this point of difference is always your first essential step.

USPs for retail ads

Your local retail stores need a USP in local newspapers or on local radio or television. It is much more "now" oriented than national consumer advertising. Price is usually a big factor here, often carrying the whole weight. More often than not, though, you'll be faced with a competitive price situation where you have to look for something else that's unique to attract attention. Some possibilities include the following:

• Special purchase (carload sale)

• Spectacular event (outdoor tent sale)

• Live celebrity demonstration

- Exclusively available

- First time available locally

- Special sale (everything 20% off)

- Special service offered (free installation)

- Promotional event (chance for a big prize)

- Borrowed interest (new-car display on shopping center mall)

- Joint promotion (lamp store and bookseller tie-in)

- Coupon offering

USPs for trade ads

Trade advertising is prepared by manufacturers and addressed to distributors, store owners, managers, or buyers in large organizations, to emphasize the benefit their *business* gains by stocking this particular brand name or product line. It's obvious that a Drexel furniture ad that appears in *Home Furnishings Daily* (profit from our well-known reputation) will differ from a Drexel ad in *Better Homes and Gardens* (built to last a lifetime—beautifully). You might find the following promises helpful when you sit down to write an ad directed to dealers:

- Faster turnover (means more money to invest again, to purchase more and to sell again)

- Attractive point-of-purchase displays available (to help dealer sell more; make more money)

- National consumer advertising support (helps presell the merchandise by making the customers more receptive; makes customers look for the item and want it)

- Cooperative advertising (manufacturer shares dealer's cost of local advertising)

- Sales incentives (makes dealer's employees more interested in the product and selling it)

- New improvement (reduces dealer's service complaints; beats competition)

- Unusual or new packaging (to catch shopper's eye, reduce spoilage, reduce breakage, reduce theft; requires less shelf space)

- Unusual profit margin (higher markup percentage than previously or higher than competition)

- Fast delivery on reorders (means more satisfied customers; special needs filled quickly)

- Unusual deals (buy 12 dozen get 1 dozen free; special discounts)

You'll find that trade advertising is heavily money oriented—how to make more money with your product. This copy psychology should be in your USP and through the entire ad. Never hide it. Shout it. There's nothing wrong with dealers (retailers) making money or making a profit; that's why they open their doors every morning!

USPs for industrial ads

Industrial advertising takes one step further back and is addressed to the manufacturers of finished products (Drexel furniture) by those who manufacturer something needed to make or market that product (fabric, tools, packaging material). When you write industrial ads, always remember the three most important things these readers are interested in:

- How to improve their product(s)

- How to be sure of a reliable source of supply

- How to cut costs (in purchasing, production, packaging)

Study your product and develop a USP that responds to one of these basic needs and you're more likely to get more response to your ads.

USPs for professional ads

Professional advertising tells professional people better ways to perform their services. Ads addressed, for example, to doctors,

INTRODUCING THE OTHER SALES FORCE
BEHIND GOLDEN BLEND™ UNDERWEAR.

Everybody knows Lou Grant, John Davidson and Fantasy Island's Mr. Roarke. But did you know we've lined up their shows to help sell underwear?

This year your customers will be seeing Golden Blend underwear all over the TV dial. On many of the highest-rated prime-time shows.

It's part of a major campaign that'll do for this brand what Union did for the Fruit of the Loom® brand.

And the support won't stop with advertising. There'll be peak season promotions to keep the sales coming all year long.

So if you don't have Golden Blend underwear, we suggest you get it. If you have it, get more. Because with a sales force like ours, and support like ours, the returns to you can only be golden.

Among those pictured above are Lou Grant and Magnum P.I. as seen on the CBS Television Network.

GOLDEN BLEND™ UNDERWEAR.
OUR FAME IS YOUR FORTUNE.

© 1981 Union Underwear Co., Inc., P.O. Box 780, Bowling Green, Kentucky 42181. An operating company of Northwest Industries.

DEALERS WELCOME ADVERTISING SUPPORT and wise manufacturers take every opportunity to tell them about the advertising program behind their products. *Courtesy Union Underwear Co., Inc.*

You're watching a glove catch a customer.

All by itself, a Louisville Slugger® glove can catch a customer. First it catches his attention with rugged good looks. And then once he's tried it on, he's caught up in a new found feeling of fielding confidence.

In fact, whether it's the big "Big Daddy" and "Big Louie" or the Steve Garvey and Graig Nettles

autograph models, you can literally see—and more importantly—feel the quality of these gloves.

Each glove in the Louisville Slugger lineup is made of top-grain cowhide. And each glove is made with the kind of craftsmanship that produces a firm yet flexible feeling of total control.

Quality is why Louisville Slugger gloves perform so well in the field. And it's why they sell through so well in your store—at solid margins.

So this season, don't order gloves catch as catch can. Order the complete Louisville Slugger line. They're the ones that sell through.

Louisville Slugger®

HsB Hillerich & Bradsby Co., Louisville, Kentucky

CONSUMER RECOGNITION of a brand name has a powerful appeal to retailers who understandably view this as a great advantage at the point of sale. *Courtesy Hillerich & Bradsby Co.*

teachers or architects feature products needed by them in the course of performing their functions. The emphasis is on how they can do their job better, faster or more effectively. While the idea of making money is obviously a factor here, it should be treated more discreetly than is necessary in industrial and dealer advertising. Seek to frame your USP in such a way that it shows professional people:

• How to improve their professionalism

• How to provide better service for their clients

• How they can be more confident in their source of supply

Building a foundation

It always helps, too, if your product or the company that makes it has already established a good reputation among those it is seeking to persuade. There's no way to measure the boost that advertising gets when people have been conditioned by experience to trust the integrity of your company. Aren't you far more inclined to try a new soup from Campbell's? Or buy a new cereal from Kellogg's? Or sample a new paper towel from Scott? The unknown company has an uphill struggle, to be sure, but success stories are not uncommon. A new product with a unique attribute that can be shown to fill a real need better than anything else available will usually prevail.

However, "unique" is not the whole answer. You have a gel toothpaste or a freeze-dried coffee. So what? The production genius who developed these products is understandably proud of the accomplishment and probably has visions of people breaking their necks in a mad rush to buy this new brain-child just as soon as it reaches the stores. But just because it's unique doesn't mean it fills a need. And any product that doesn't is dead. Uniqueness alone is not a reason to buy. What you're searching for is a *Unique* Selling Proposition. It must motivate people to buy.

In other words, people aren't very likely to buy a toothpaste in a gel form until they're convinced that, for some reason or other, it helps to prevent decay. People can't be expected to buy coffee just because it's made by a new freeze-drying process until they're convinced that it puts better flavor in the cup (so

Goodyear rubber railroad crossing pads help this auto maker protect auto parts.

Back and forth, back and forth, all day long, vehicles scurry across these tracks. They're laden with heavy engines, delicate parts, fenders and fuel tanks. All on specially designed carts, wagons and trucks.

To protect the vehicles as well as the cargo, the plant maintenance manager had Goodyear rubber railroad crossing pads put in. That was back in 1969. The crossing has performed so well, with such little maintenance required, that this plant is adding more Goodyear crossings.

The reasons are obvious. Traffic, even the kind with small diameter wheels, zips across the tracks without a jolt. There's no breakage or spillage, traffic is smoother and faster.

If you have a crossing that's tearing up your fork lifts, jolting and breaking up cargo, give Don Johnson, Product Engineer, a call, (419) 394-3311 or write Goodyear, Box 52, Akron, OH 44309.

We know how to help.

GOOD YEAR
INDUSTRIAL PRODUCTS

A PROMISE OF LOWER COSTS hits home with manufacturing companies which are constantly seeking ways to keep costs under control so their products aren't overpriced. *Courtesy Goodyear Tire & Rubber Co.*

A leading polish.   Pledge.

Unretouched photograph

"My table proved it...
Pledge makes a beautiful difference."

"I tested Pledge® against a popular polish on my dining room table, and look at the results! This unretouched photo proves that Pledge does more to bring out the beauty of the wood.
Pledge picks up dust...cleans up fingerprints, dirt and smudges...and lets the wood grain come shining through.
I just can't see myself using anything but Pledge."

**Pledge brings out the beauty.
Every time you dust.**

A UNIQUE BENEFIT is reinforced by a dramatic visual demonstration that provides all the proof necessary to support the headline claim. *Courtesy S. C. Johnson & Son, Inc.*

that the user will personally enjoy the coffee more and probably get compliments from the group at next week's dinner). And don't you do the same thing when the roles are reversed and you're the buyer and not the seller? Aren't you always asking yourself, "What's in it for me?" Just because something is different doesn't necessarily make it better—or mean you need it. All of this is plain common sense, to be sure. But altogether too often common sense gets sidetracked in the rush to be "creative." If it shows in the advertising, it's too bad.

You're looking for uniqueness and for a selling proposition, and the latter is probably more important than the former. Never lose sight of the fact that *while marketers are selling products and services, people are buying benefits.* It is absolutely essential that a Unique Selling Proposition be stated in terms that people relate to and can apply to their own perceived needs. The ideal USP makes an offer that, as the saying goes, can't be refused.

Now, what about the gel toothpaste and the freeze-dried coffee? What finally happened was that the gel was given credit as a new kind of carrier for whitening and mouthwash ingredients: the product was claimed to be one that cleaned teeth and freshened breath at the same time. The gel form made the product look new and different. The advertising made this new feature (which of itself was unimportant) accountable for a clear benefit (which responded to a need felt by consumers). A *unique* form was translated into a meaningful *selling proposition.* If it hadn't been done, the advertising would have had no punch at all.

In the case of the coffee, freeze-drying was equated with flavor-saving. It wasn't just a technical achievement but a technical achievement that made possible a more flavorful cup of coffee. That's all the coffee drinkers were interested in. The process was meaningless, from a marketing viewpoint, until it was connected to a genuine benefit.

People think mainly of themselves, of their own satisfactions, their own gratifications and their own enhancement. Their own needs and wants are uppermost in their minds. So don't be deceived by the great new product or innovation or technological breakthrough that you're now about to announce to the world. It means nothing from a sales point of view until you can prove to a prospective buyer that it's something he or she really needs for some reason or another. Do *you* buy things you don't think you'll need? Why should the people you're talking to act any differently?

So the Unique Selling Proposition is the base that supports the advertising you'll be creating. You wouldn't attempt to build a house without a foundation, would you? Despite this obvious conclusion, too much advertising looks like it was done by somebody ignoring the obvious. For proof, all you have to do is open a copy of today's newspaper. Too much advertising, as noted before, talks to itself.

It may seem somewhat of an oversimplification to place so much emphasis on developing a Unique Selling Proposition. Nothing could be further from the truth. Isn't that ounce of gold worth the tons of ore that must be mined to obtain it? And a strong USP is the ounce of gold that results from the following inputs:

- Your knowledge of the product (how it's made, what it does and why) or service (how it differs from others).

- Your understanding of the target audience (age, sex, income—everything).

- Your understanding of the market (sales trends, competition, case histories of other products in the category).

- Your personal experience (there's no substitute for experience, but even a beginner with an average amount of common sense can quickly learn to locate the "on" button).

AIDA

Now that you have your head and desk crammed full of research about the product, the target, features, benefits and Unique Selling Propositions, how do you start to put your ad together? There's a classic formula for assembling a good ad—AIDA (see chart on p. 62):

A stands for *attention*. If you don't pull this off, that elusive reader flips right past you. In most cases your USP will provide the basis for grabbing the reader's attention. Don't forget such trigger words as NEW, NOW, AT LAST, FINALLY, AMAZING, FREE, HOW TO, SUDDENLY. They work.

I stands for *interest.* After you've flagged down your reader you've got to come up with something that will hold his or her interest or, whoops, the page (or dial) is turned.

D stands for *desire.* So far, so good. You've managed to stop the reader and get him or her involved. Now it's time to make that reader smack his or her lips for what it is you're selling.

A stands for *action.* No need to belabor this point. If an ad doesn't move a reader to go out and get your product—or feel favorably inclined to buy it at some future time when the need arises—it has failed. Convincing people of the superiority of your product—or position—is the name of the game. Nothing else matters. Period.

Anyone who has ever sat through an advertising course in school or college is familiar with this formula. And yes, it's necessary to refer back to it from time to time because it's altogether too easy to stray from the straight and narrow in the name of "creativity."

TWO SIMPLE RULES

If you were able to reduce all the rules from all the books about writing advertising down to an absolute, bare-bones minimum, these two would remain:

1. An ad must be simple.

2. An ad must look like it's worthwhile to pay attention to.

Any advertising that doesn't meet this bare minimum is likely to be overlooked and ignored. Do *you* look at or listen to advertising that is confusing or boring or both? And an ad doesn't have to be big and fancy to measure up, either. Those tiny newspaper ads for "Hemorrhoid Sufferers" get outstanding readership, year after year. Why? Because they're the soul of simplicity and because they seem very worthwhile to that segment of the population most likely to buy the product.

Of course, you say. But just wait until you take your USP and start to translate it into real advertising! You'll be tempted to make it more "complete" (translation: to contain more than one idea). Others will often urge you to "add a point about . . ." Even the advertiser will sometimes request that you introduce another fact or feature. It happens all the time, even in the biggest agencies and with the most sophisticated advertisers. Resist at all costs!

Meddlers who offer suggestions have delusions about the way advertising works. They labor under the impression that everybody out there is as avidly interested in their product as they are. That unless each ad is a catalog of all the product's virtues, somehow the advertiser is not getting his money's worth. Far from helping an ad, any "extras" like this are distracting and undermine its impact.

Always keep things simple.

POSITIVE VS. NEGATIVE

How many times has someone said, "Don't do this or don't do that."? Most people object to being told what they can't do simply because they heard it too much as a child, and it seems to block their freedom. Tell your target what it *can do;* what your product *can do.* Avoid telling what your product cannot do with such "weak negatives" as "won't," "can't," "don't" and "doesn't."

As with all rules, there will be exceptions. But keep the exceptions to a minimum and you won't dilute the impact when the right moment comes. And certainly you'll keep words such as "never," "avoid," "stop," and "reduce" in your arsenal. These are *strong* negatives as compared to the *weak* negatives noted earlier. The distinction is important.

Why make such a big thing about this? A successful salesman tries to get his customers to think "Yes." He builds his sales presentation on trying to get the customer to agree, to be in a "yes" frame of mind—and eventually to get the order, he hopes! Why, then, should you as a copywriter start to plant "no" in your reader's mind when you are really trying just as hard as the salesman for a "yes" frame of reference? Why plant the word "no" at all?

And remember this: unlike the personal salesman engaged in person-to-person selling, you're not physically there to play the devil's advocate with your "soft sell" negative techniques.

There are other reasons for emphasizing the positive in your copywriting. A negative explanation often is more involved than a simple, straightforward, positive approach. Sometimes the negative approach will totally turn off your target.

Sometimes it takes some extra thought and effort to "write around" a weak negative and turn the sentence into a positive statement. But try it. You can avoid weak negatives if you try: "don't forget" means "remember." "Don't miss this great opportunity" means "Get in on this great opportunity." Think about this ad from Alcoholics Anonymous: "Want to drink? That's your business. Want to stop? That's our business." All positive. No weak negatives.

What all advertising tries to do is win someone's favor, to get people to agree with what the ad proposes. To make this come about, you must do everything in your power to put your audience in a frame of mind that will be receptive to what you're suggesting. The right psychological setting is essential if you're to succeed. The wrong picture can mean instant rebuke. The wrong tone of voice can be fatal. The wrong word can trigger a chain reaction that leads to rejection. It's worth all the time it takes to avoid these misfortunes because, yes, they are avoidable.

Basic
writing style

5

Advertising copywriting is a world unto itself. The grammar gospel preached in classrooms is breached as often as it's observed. "Nobody can do it like McDonald's can!" boasts the fast-food giant. "Ain't no reason to go anyplace else!" responds an aggressive competitor. Language purists can only wince and bear it. Such usage is accepted because it's effective. One-word sentences, sentences starting with a conjunction, run-on sentences, dangling participles—the copywriter's arsenal is loaded with weapons that once were taboo, and still are in academic circles.

The thing to remember is that the writing style of the copywriter is very pragmatic: if it works, it's good.

CLARITY

Clarity is the name of the game. The obscure, the merely "clever" that draws attention to itself, the profound—these have no place in advertising. The casual reader or listener must grasp instantly the idea you're trying to convey. A person might be willing to ponder a play or book or motion picture, but an ad earns no such second thoughts. It has just one chance. It must be understood—now! When clarity collides with grammar, guess which one wins? "Nobody can do it *as* McDonald's can" might be correct, but it's not as quick, It's schoolbookish, stuffy, a turnoff. "Like," on the other hand, is relaxed, easy, natural. It also suggests a positive idea, "liking," in a subtle way. Advertising words have to work hard; you seize gratefully any extra edge you can find. You can be sure the copywriter knew the correct word for the McDonald's line, but its livelier alternative was better advertising. It was no contest. No other choice could have been made.

Even so, you're making a big mistake if you take this freedom as license to brutalize the English language. Exceptions are only powerful as long as they're exceptions—part of their power comes from their very unexpectedness. Most of the time you'll follow the rules of grammar, punctuation and composition learned in school. Only when the rulebook answer seems to slow the reader, when it seems weak, awkward or uncomfortable does it yield to a choice that's strong, positive, natural. If nothing else, the language of advertising is a living language: current, modern, reflecting the crosscurrents that toss us to and fro in our daily lives. The language of advertising is vernacular, not literary. That's what often makes it colorful—and clear.

And if it's any consolation, the people who scold advertising for its frequent abandonment of traditional rules are often the very same people who are so influenced by it when they assume their other roles: parents, homeowners, shoppers. Copywriters learn to suffer barbs gladly when they know their words are working.

TEN TIMELY TIPS

The following tips are not rules but merely some sound advice you might want to keep in mind as you proceed. The list sums up many of the observations made above. After awhile you'll develop your own list. You may work for clients who have their own thoughts about the subject. Some of these ideas are obvious, but they are always worth repeating. (Which is altogether appropriate since repetition is one of the tools of your trade!) You'll find these tips worth referring to from time to time:

- Make it easy on your reader. Write short sentences. Use easy, familiar words. (See "The Writing Yardstick," p. 83.)

- Don't waste words. Say what you have to say—nothing more, nothing less. Don't pad, but don't skimp. If it takes a thousand words, use a thousand words. As long as not one is excess baggage.

- Stick to the present tense, active voice—it's crisper. Avoid the past tense and passive voice—these forms tend to drag. Exceptions should be deliberate, for special effect.

- Don't hesitate to use personal pronouns. Remember, you're trying to talk to just *one* person so talk as you would to a friend. Use "you" and "your."

- Cliches are crutches; learn to get along without them. Bright, surprising words and phrases perk up readers, keep them reading.

- Don't overpunctuate. It kills copy flow. Excessive commas are the chief culprits. Don't give your readers any excuse to jump ship.

- Use contractions whenever possible. They're fast, personal, natural. People talk in contractions. (Listen to yourself.)

- Don't brag or boast. Everyone hates a bore. Translate those product features you're so proud of into consumer benefits that ring the bell with your readers. Write from the reader's point of view, not your own. Avoid "we," "us," "our."

- Be single-minded. Don't try to do too much. If you chase more than one rabbit at a time, you'll catch none.

- Write with flair. Drum up excitement. Make sure the enthusiasm you feel comes through in your copy.

CHOPPY COPY

As a writer you're weaving a web. It's always very fragile. One wrong move and everything comes apart. Worse, your prey slips away. You've succeeded in attracting the attention of the reader with your headline. Now the seduction starts. You want to draw this reader through the copy. All the way.

Choppy copy puts all this in peril. If your thoughts jump around, the reader will jump off. One sentence must flow smoothly into the next. The reader must *want* to stay with you, must feel that he or she will miss something important by dropping off too soon. But what do you do when you have much to say and no time to resort to the niceties that a novelist always has handy? There are ways. An advertising copywriter soon develops tricks of the trade to handle this problem. What tricks? For instance:

- One-word transitions. Where there is chop or lack of flow between sentences, start the second sentence with *and, but, yes, plus, because, best of all.* Another way to create this one-word transition is to start the second sentence with an adjective, which often will force you to shift your sentence structure. Starting your second sentence with a verb form also helps.

- Enumerate the copy points you want to make. This lets you be brief. Besides, people tend to be led along by a series of numbers.

- Ask a question. This neatly solicits the facts you're going to provide anyhow.

- Dot your way out. If you don't overdo it, the use of the elipsis (. . .) can easily carry you into the next point.

Every copywriter also has favorite ways to slip out of tight spots. Before long you'll have your own. Still, the above list has proven very handy over the years for many copywriters.

THE WRITING YARDSTICK
A tool for more effective writing*

This yardstick indicates how difficult or easy it is to understand your letters, reports, and other writing. It is based on a scale for measuring reading difficulty developed by Dr. Rudolf Flesch and adapted for use at The Prudential. The scale is explained in detail in "The Art of Plain Talk," which was published by Harper & Row and copyrighted in 1946 by Dr. Flesch. These factors are involved:

- The *more words* in a sentence, the *more difficult* it is to read and understand that sentence.

- The *more syllables* a word has, the *more difficult* it is to read and understand that word.

- The *more personal references* in a passage, the *easier* it is to read and understand that passage.

The last line of the yardstick lists reading matter at each of several levels. The "standard" writing level is easily understood by most persons.

How to use the writing yardstick

- Unless you want to test a complete letter or report, select several samples of about 100 words each, preferably not from the introduction or conclusion.

- Count the words in the samples. Then count the sentences. Divide the number of words by the number of sentences. Count contractions and hyphenated words as one word. Numbers and letters separated by spaces should be regarded as single words. In counting sentences, tabulate each unit of thought as a sentence even though it is set off by colons or semicolons rather than periods.

* Adapted from "Appendix: How to Use the Yardstick Formula" in Rudolf Flesch, *The Art of Plain Talk*, Copyright, 1946 by Rudolf Flesch. By permission of Harper & Row, Publishers, Inc. Courtesy: The Prudential Insurance Company of America.

GUIDEPOSTS TO MORE EFFECTIVE WRITING

- Shorten your sentences to an average of 17 words.
- Shorten your words so that they average about 150 syllables for each 100 words.
- Use about six personal references per 100 words.

Reading Level	Very Easy	Easy	Fairly Easy	Standard	Fairly Difficult	Difficult	Very Difficult
Average Sentence Length in Words	8	11	14	17	21	25	29
Syllables Per 100 Words	127	134	142	150	158	166	175
Personal References Per 100 Words	19	14	10	6	4	3	2
Typical Magazines	Comics	Pulp	Time	Reader's Digest	Literary	Scholarly	Scientific and Professional

• Count the syllables in the samples. Divide the total by the number of words and multiply the result by 100. The result is the number of syllables for each 100 words. This, of course, is a rough measure. A more detailed test is described in *The Art of Plain Talk*.

• Count the personal references. Divide the total by the number of words and multiply the result by 100. This gives the number of references per 100 words. There are three types of personal references:

Personal pronouns, such as I, you, he, she, them, me, himself, ourselves, and yourselves.

Names of people. Count the entire name, including any title, as one reference.

Words referring to human beings or human relationships. Count only the following: aunt, baby, boy, brother, child, cousin, dad, daddy, dame, daughter, family, father, fellow, folks, friend, gentlemen, girl, guy, husband, kid, lad, lady, lass, madam, mama, man, miss, mister, mother, nephew, niece, pal, poppa, parent, people (not peoples), sir, sister, son, sweetheart, uncle, wife, woman. Count as one personal reference combinations of these words such as baby boy and girl friend and combinations using grand-, great-, step- and -in-law.

COPYREADING SYMBOLS

While a copywriter should be able to handle a typewriter to some degree, nobody expects you to be a perfect typist. You will make errors. What you must be able to do is convey any corrections clearly. The following list of the more familiar symbols is widely accepted and should help give a professional look to your rough-typed copy.

Note the use of the caret (an upside-down V) to indicate something is to be inserted. Also, often the new copy to be inserted is placed in a "half moon." This is important so there is no doubt where your correction goes, particularly when there is more than one correction on the same line.

CORRECTION TO BE MADE	HOW TO MAKE IT
1. Insert a period	1. Run to the store⊗
2. Insert a dash	2. Pause⌄then go
3. Insert a hyphen	3. A full⌃time job
4. Start a new paragraph	4. ⌊Billy went to his
5. Make small letter a capital letter (upper case)	5. henry likes
6. Make capital letter a small letter (lower case)	6. Why Ⱡot go with
7. Combine two sentences into one	7. How can he go⸞ And b here too?
8. Transpose order of letters	8. Ma⁀yr
9. Transpose order of words	9. He ⁀come will ⁀
10. Add a comma	10. Fish, meat⸜fruit
11. Add an apostrophe	11. It⌄s
12. Close up space in word	12. Mississi⌢ppi
13. Close up space between words	13. Henry went in ⌢in the
14. Delete a letter	14. Bett⌢ly likes to
15. Add space between letters	15. Jane⁁nd Mary went
16. Change a letter in word	16. Pat went tonig⌃t
17. Change an entire word	17. Throw ~~them~~ a bat
18. To indicate no paragraph	18. Henry went too.⸩ ⸤Next time it⸩ ⸤rained.

19. To indicate end of copy

19. # or numeral 30

20. To indicate more copy on next page

20. (More)

21. Spell out the word

21. He lives in (Pa.)

22. Change word to an abbreviation

22. The (United States) is

23. Change number to numerals

23. He must be (forty)

24. Spell out numerals as a word

24. Over (30) pages long

25. If you change your mind and want original word printed

25. why he ~~went~~ *stet* is hard to

26. Set in boldface type

26. I said to hurry to go

27. Add leader dots

27. Why not if (x)(x)(x)

Basic print techniques

6

For years you have been reading advertisements like most people—as a consumer. Now start to read them as someone interested in being the creator of those advertisements—a copywriter.

ANATOMY OF PRINT ADS

Start to take ads apart to see the various elements that make them what they are. Start to practice identifying the elements so you will be able to use them yourself in your own arrangements as a creator of advertising. Some of the elements you already know and immediately recognize. Others may be new to you, or at least new to you from a copywriter's viewpoint. You have seen these elements for years but now start to study them, to study advertisements!

Here are the eight basic elements you'll be working with:

- *Headline.* (Or simply Hed in copywriter's shorthand). Typically, it's the largest type in an advertisement. Used for *strong emphasis; very dramatic.*

- *Subhead.* (Subhed). Next to the largest type size; of *medium* dramatic strength in your ad.

- *Body Copy.* (Text). Explains ideas in more detail. It is of smaller size and less intensity than either the Hed or Subhed.

- *Illustration.* (Pix). Any picture used in the advertisement, either photograph or artist's drawing.

- *Caption.* Words in smaller type directly under or next to an illustration; used to *explain* the illustration.

- *Price.* Used when necessary if the price is of dominant size and if *not* directly part of another element.

- *Logotype.* (Logo). Any product, corporate or store name that is *always* set in a *particular typeface* or with a particular trade character or design motif, such as the special script type always used for Coca-Cola.

- *Signature.* (Sig). Any product, corporate or store name that is set in any typeface that the artist or newspaper production department desires to use.

These are the eight key elements you will think about as a copywriter for print media. They should be sufficient to describe the anatomy of any advertisement in a newspaper, magazine, direct mail piece or other printed advertising material. They are not only helpful to describe an ad but are vital in your *internal* communication efforts, described in the next section.

Your next step is putting these elements in place so they do their job. The Headline is the star. It should get most of your attention. Not only is it set largest (usually!) but it often is all a person takes time to read. Its role is to state a benefit so persuasively that the reader is moved to continue rather than turn the page.

What's read next is the Subhead (set slightly smaller) or the ad's Text (even smaller) if there is no Subhead. Remember, every ad doesn't always contain every element. Your job is not simply to assemble the elements, like jigsaw puzzle pieces, until the ad is complete. Your job is to try to make certain a reader sticks with you from top (Headline) to bottom (Logo or Signature) so that he or she wants the product and is prepared to take the next step—buying it.

As mentioned previously, it's important for a copywriter to be able to visualize his or her completed ad. Why is this necessary? Because, remember, the entire job starts with you, the copywriter. You'll usually have an artist help you with your professional art needs, but your own copywriter's visualization is important. You will be doing your visualizing in terms of these elements just described.

And don't be surprised to realize you can have more than one Subhead in an ad, more than one Text area, more than one Logo (especially in a retail ad where product Logos appear as well as the store Logo). There will even be times when you choose to use more than one Headline—or none at all. Everything hinges on your judgement as a copywriter of what is important in your ad to get the message across.

Many ads have been written with merely a large photograph and very few words. For years it took just two words to sell a female sanitary product: "Modess because . . ." And "This is Marlboro Country" had a good long run for the cigarette maker. When it comes to outdoor advertising, the traditional formula is a big illustration and headline—and that's all. See pages 46–47.

INTERNAL COMMUNICATION

Usually many newspapers will let you write all your local retail copy directly on your Visual Sheet (layout). But most advertising agencies and advertising departments in corporations prefer a *typewritten* Copy Sheet and *separate* layout.

In the last section you were formally introduced or reintroduced to the various elements in the anatomy of an advertisement. You have been aware of them for years as a reader of print advertising in newspapers, magazines, counter cards, mailing pieces and catalogs. They are basic to print media. You will use these elements to communicate with the various people who must either approve your work as a copywriter or people who will help you produce your advertisement. These approval steps for your ad will differ depending on your own organization's policies.

For local retail advertising appearing in local newspapers, the approval is usually fast and easy compared to the approval steps required for your copy in most advertising agencies or corporate advertising departments. Rarely do you enjoy the luxury of being the approving authority for your own work. Usually you are writing for the approval of someone else within your own organization or outside it—copy supervisor, advertising director, sales manager, client.

On the production side of your internal communication problem you will want to communicate your thoughts and visualization effectively to the artist, to your own production department, and to a printer, depending on how large your organization is. If it is small you may be communicating directly with a printer. This internal communication of your ideas is very important.

Proper use of the advertising elements and the format for your internal communication often will determine whether you miss deadlines, have to do the job over, wait for type corrections, wait for mechanical corrections, must rerun a newspaper ad at your newspaper's expense (known as a "make good") or increase your corporation's or agency's typesetting charges due to your author's alterations.

You must be able to communicate not only to the world "outside" your profession (the world of potential consumers) but *internally* as well. A copywriter must be a careful, disciplined communicator. And this is where it all starts, with the *internal* detailing of your job. That "great idea" is not enough in this business of copywriting. You'll first have to communicate that great idea internally on a Copy Sheet.

Here is where you first put your ad down on paper. You've studied the problem, you're familiar with the product, you know what the competition's saying. Now you're about to submit your ideas on a sheet of paper—for the scrutiny of others. All those thoughts buzzing around in your brain are about to make an appearance, to take shape and form. It's a crucial moment for every copywriter, young or old.

COPY SHEET

The illustration (p. 93) shows the proper spacing on your typewriter to complete a Copy Sheet. Be sure to give special attention to how the Pix element is shown; each illustration is briefly described. Be sure to put parentheses ( ) around your description to avoid having the description set in type.

Also notice there is no effort on your Copy Sheet to try to design the ad on your typewriter as it will appear in printed form. This "design of your ad" will be shown on your Visual Sheet that *goes along with* your Copy Sheet and which will be described shortly. The only time you design on your typewriter is when you have *very strong* feelings, as the copywriter, that you want certain copy on separate lines. Then do type it on separate lines. Otherwise, let the artist or production staff worry about things like the length of the lines, size of type and type style.

The only purpose of your Copy Sheet is *to get you the type you need* for your completed ad. Whatever words are in your ad must be on your Copy Sheet. This includes such information as "a division of Schrumach Products, Inc." where necessary. All trademark symbols (TM) and all copyright symbols © must also be on your Copy Sheet in proper position.

The first element entry on your Copy Sheet is *the element that is at the top of your ad* in *your own mental visualization.* So you can see this can be any element you desire depending on how you are starting the ad. All the other elements then follow in order on your Copy Sheet from top to bottom of your visualization. Hence, at the top of your ad could be a Subhed with the Hed at the bottom of the ad! Nothing wrong with that at all. How do *you* visualize your ad? What weight are *you* giving the different words and illustrations? You can have a Copy Sheet without any headline or without captions or without text areas or without illustrations. Your Copy Sheet reflects the ad you are working on and nothing else. Do not show any element entries for elements you are not using.

Here are a few explanations about physical requirements on your Copy Sheet:

• Always use standard 8½ x 11 typing paper; never use onion skin paper. Use one side only.

```
CLIENT: Sweet Tooth
MEDIUM: Altoona Star Ledger          COPYWRITER'S NAME_____
SIZE:   4 x 10
INSERTION DATE: 5/6                  DATE_____
```

Subhed: (10 spaces) Now, just in time for Mother's Day...
                    _____ 3 spaces

Hed: delicious candy at ½ price!
                    _____ 3 spaces

Pix: (mother opening box of candy)

Text: Remember your Mother this Mother's Day in the
                    _____ 2 spaces
                   sweetest way. With candy. Fresh and beautifully
                    _____ 2 spaces
                   wrapped, it makes a most welcome gift... and

                   without size problems!

Pix: (2 boxes of candy on sale)

Caption: 2 lbs., regularly $7 now $3.50

Caption: 4 lbs., regularly $12 now $6

Text: Hurry in today. Supply limited. Use your

                   convenient Sweet Tooth charge or handy Bankall

                   Charge Card.

Logo: Sweet Tooth

                   1901 N. Main Street

COPY SHEET: Each element appears in the order you see it in your
own mental visualization of the ad. Note spacing; don't crowd copy.
Elements must be reentered by name whenever there is a type-size
change in your visualization.

• Triple space between elements.

• Double space within the element.

• Allow five spaces for your left margin; then type your *element identification.* Allow ten spaces to start the *actual copy* for your first element. Line up all other element identifications and copy under your first entry, as shown.

You'll notice the heading information to identify the ad is single spaced in the upper part of your Copy Sheet. Drop down at least three lines before starting actual copy.

At the end of your Copy Sheet use the symbol # or the number 30. This means "the end." If you have to type your copy on more than one page for the same job, type the word "more" at the end of that page in parentheses or circle it. Continuation pages have this information at the top of the page in one continuous line: your last name/production number/client's name/short title of the job/size/page number of Copy Sheet.

There's no need to erase on your Copy Sheet. Just xxxx-out your error and type it correctly. If you catch errors after you have finished, correct your error in pencil using the copyreader symbols on p. 86. Never use pen or ink for corrections. Nobody expects you to be a perfect typist. Avoid breaking parts of the same element between two pages. Start the whole thing on the next page. (This even applies to paragraphs; the entire paragraph should be on the same page.) Never type on the back of a page.

Once you have mastered identifying the different elements, you can visualize your ad and can communicate your ideas on an easily understood Copy Sheet.

DOODLE

You're not an artist. Nobody expects you to be. But you must be able to visualize the work you create. Chances are you'll see in your own mind the way you'd like your ad to look. Now you have to communicate this idea to the artist or art director who will be responsible for designing the layout. You'll probably find it helpful to do a doodle layout that you'll take along for guidance. At a glance, the art director will see what you have in mind,

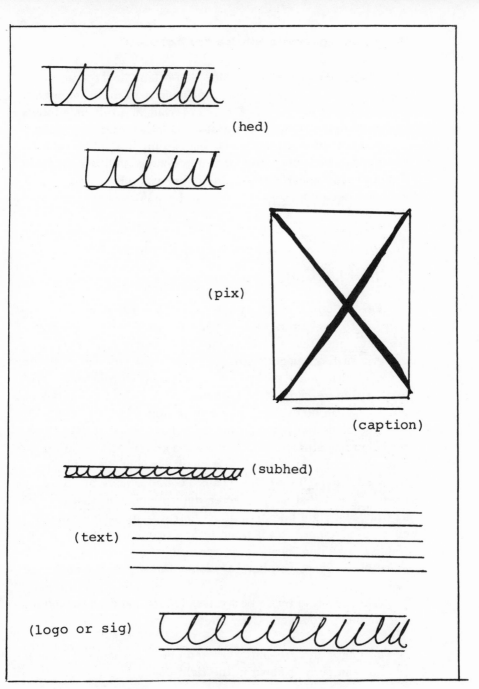

(hed)

(pix)

(caption)

(subhed)

(text)

(logo or sig)

COPYWRITER'S DOODLE: This type of visual sheet can be used for magazine and direct mail advertising because it is done in an advertising agency or corporate advertising department where there are artists to help you. It will not be sufficient for newspaper copywriting. Never show this to a client; minimum to be shown to a client is a *rough layout* (see p. 97). Note: element names are on this example for your information only; they do not go on your Doodle.

what you're trying to convey. More important, he'll see the value you've given the various elements—which are more important, which are less important. A doodle layout like this probably is the only—and certainly the fastest—way to transmit this information to your art partner so he or she can pitch in and help.

In any event, this kind of simple doodle is all that's usually required of a copywriter in an agency or corporate ad department where competent art people are on the staff—maybe right next door.

ROUGH LAYOUT

On the other hand, a rough layout is what is normally required of copywriters writing copy for local, retail newspaper accounts. Since this is a fairly common experience for advertising writers, all the aspects of rough layouts that you can easily do yourself are included in this section. Naturally a professional artist can do a more competent job. But you will be surprised how much you can do even without any artistic ability.

If your newspaper does not have blank pads of paper with the column widths already premeasured and ruled, then just measure off the size of your ad on a blank piece of 8½ x 11 paper. If the ad is to be 3 x 10, this means 3 columns *wide* by 10 inches *deep*. It's just that simple. After determining the size of your ad draw a straight line *around all four sides* of your ad to mark off its dimensions. This is done to keep your visualization from "falling apart" or "floating" in space. It also gives you a better grasp of the space you have available; the size of the challenge facing you.

Next, neatly letter, as best you can in freehand, all the following elements from your Copy Sheet:

- all Logos (if a previously printed one is available, just cut it out and paste it down in the right place)

- all Signatures (same instructions as above)

- all Headlines

- all Subheads (when major in size)

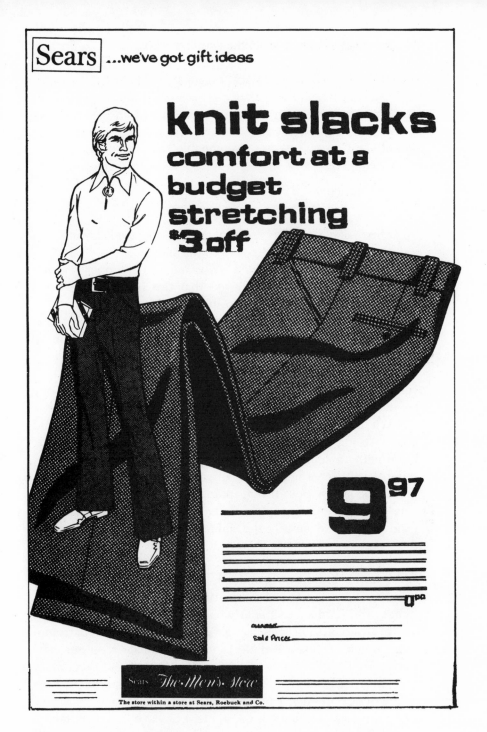

ROUGH LAYOUT: Rendered by an artist, and is the next step after a
Copywriter's Doodle. *Courtesy Sears Roebuck and Co.*

• all Prices (when important, bigger than Text size)

Then, indicate with neat, horizontal, ruled lines:

• all Text areas (rule in a "reasonable" area based on amount of copy)

• all Captions

Minor-size Subheads are shown on your rough layout with a dark wavy line between two straight lines.

The Pix element is glued or waxed in its proper position on the layout. You can easily see that this newspaper "Visual Sheet" is fast turning into a passable rough layout.

Be sure to identify your rough layout with the same information as on your Copy Sheet. *Do not* put this information inside the ad you have just created; this identification information goes on the upper part of the sheet. The information is needed on your rough layout in case it becomes separated from your Copy Sheet.

When you have completed your first rough layout, it should give a strong indication of what the finished ad will look like. Even without containing all the copy on your Copy Sheet, your rough layout for a newspaper ad should be able to do a strong selling job all by itself. If not, something probably is wrong with your basic selling concepts for the ad. This is an easy, fast and good way to test quickly the selling power of your ad. Look at the rough layout by itself. Does it sell? Does it have a Unique Selling Proposition? Capture attention?

Your rough layout is, indeed, a blueprint that can be read by your client and by others on the staff who will now be able to help you produce on paper what you visualized in your head.

In an advertising agency or corporate advertising department these rough layouts are done by a professional artist. See how they start to sell even without a Copy Sheet? But remember that on a local newspaper you can easily be required to be a copywriter, a "pseudo artist" and, of course, an account executive too! Although you may not be an artist or have much art talent, you can always try to be neat.

ROUGH LAYOUT: This makes use of "clip art" (see p. 110) provided by manufacturer or art service. This will actually be the artwork that appears in the finished ad.

```
CLIENT:  Polaroid Corp.
MEDIUM:  St. Louis Nsp          COPYWRITER'S NAME_____
SIZE:    3½" x 6"
INSERTION DATE:  12/16          DATE_____
```

(A) Pix: (2 packs T108 tied with ribbon)

(B) Hed: A great gift idea
                        for under $00.

(C) Text: Give someone two packs of Polaroid
                        color film for Christmas -- and watch
                        it turn into 16 instant Christmas
                        gifts. Or get some for yourself...
                        and hear everybody say: "Let's take
                        some more!"

(D) Box: Type 108 Colorpack Land film $0.00 per pack.
                        Type 88 for Square Shooters $0.00 per pack.

(E) Logo: Dealer Name

(F) Copy: Polaroid (R) by Polaroid Corporation

COPY SHEET WITH KEYED COPY: Each of the elements is identified
by letter for reference on the rough layout. *Courtesy Polaroid Corporation.*

KEYING

"Keying" is how a copywriter indicates to an art director exactly what goes where on a layout: each ad element is identified on both the Copy Sheet and rough layout (see following pages). The Copy Sheet contains every word that will be contained in the ad—including such small but important items as copyright and trademark statements that are absolutely essential. Such fine points need not be keyed on the rough layout; the fact that they are typed on the Copy Sheet is sufficient to assure that this material will be set in type and not forgotten.

While some newspapers allow you to put all your copy directly on the layout, the common practice is to coordinate copy and layout with alphabetical keys to make the position of each element readily apparent.

Keying is easy providing you do it *after* you finish your Copy Sheet and visual sheet. Just follow these steps:

- On your Copy Sheet, jot the key letters in the left-hand margin alongside the element designation. Circle each key.

- Use the letter A to key the first element typed on your Copy Sheet (not necessarily the Headline). Proceed through the alphabet for your keys.

- Follow this placement pattern on your visual sheet. Key all Headlines, Subheads that are lettered in, Pix, Prices, Sig and Logos to the *left* of where they appear. Key Text and Captions *inside* the indicated area.

- Text areas that follow in order on your Copy Sheet are keyed only once. If the Text blocks jump around, each Text block must get a separate key that indicates its proper placement on your visual sheet.

- If the *size* of the type in the text *varies* in your mind (visualization), be sure you assign a separate key for each different size because each is a separate visual element in the layout.

- Key the advertiser's name, address, phone number and any regularly used slogan on both the Copy Sheet and rough layout.

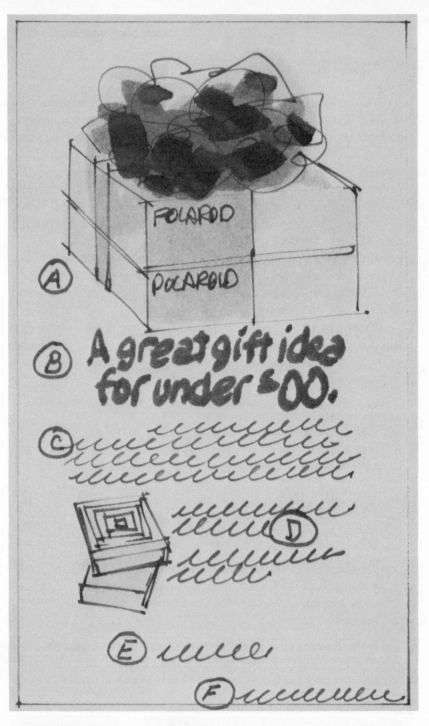

ROUGH LAYOUT WITH KEYED COPY: Using the clearly marked letter keys, there's no mistaking where each element goes. *Courtesy Polaroid Corporation.*

MAKING YOUR JOB EASIER

Resist the temptation to design your ad in your typewriter; that's what your visual sheet is for. Just type your copy in the normal way across the Copy Sheet. If you have a strong desire for certain copy to appear on separate lines on the layout, be sure to type it on separate lines. This will normally apply only to Heads and Subheads.

And be sure to keep a copy of your Copy Sheet. Never part with your last copy of *anything*. There's nothing more frustrating than recomposing a piece of copy that got lost along the way. Be smart. Hang on to everything you write. It's a lot easier than doing it all over again.

It will help keep track of things if you get in the habit of typing "(More)" at the bottom of each page of a job, except the last page, of course. Type the character # or the number 30 to indicate the end. Also, make sure that each additional page is suitably identified in case the pages get separated along the way, a not-unlikely possibility when you consider all the people who are involved in the production process of an ad.

As far as the type itself goes, it will be comforting to know that you can rely on experts to take care of it. Either the artist you're working with or the production department (depending on exactly where you're working) will "spec" (pronounced *speck*) your type, which means specify the appropriate size after checking the length of the copy and the space available on the layout. Therefore, there is no need for the copywriter to be overly concerned about "copy-fitting." Just be reasonable.

Rather than counting type characters and space counts, study some newspaper and magazine ads; you'll very quickly get a strong feeling for the amount of space needed for different type sizes. If you're liberal with the use of white space in your visualization of the ad, you should have no serious problems.

DESIGN

This section is in no way intended to make you an artist. The words "design," "layout," "visual sheet" or "artist" are used here only in the broadest sense.

"Coca-Cola" and "Coke"

Trade-mark®   Trade-mark®

Our trade-marks have endured stock market crashes, world wars, the nuclear age, and would be imitators.

But can they endure the typewriter?

Ahh, that's the key to our survival!

For the typewriter has many means of destroying us.

For example, there's the hideous torture of being lower cased to death.

Or the painful demise of strangulation through pluralization.

Or, worse yet, the agony of being stretched on the rack of the possessive.

These are the nightmares which keep our lawyers awake and trembling at night. They're strong, courageous men, who will go beyond the call of duty to protect our trade-marks. But alas, even a trade-mark lawyer has his breaking point.

So please. Watch your typewriter. All you need remember is our simple trade-mark rule: **"Always capitalized, never pluralized, never possessive."**

The Coca-Cola Company

TRADEMARK PROTECTION is an ongoing project at many companies that own such valuable properties. To be lax in this regard could lead to loss of the trademark. *Courtesy The Coca-Cola Company, owner and registrant of the trademarks Coca-Cola and Coke. In Canada, Coca-Cola Ltd. is the registered owner of the trademarks Coca-Cola and Coke.*

The fact remains, however, that even though you're a copy-writer, you're dealing in the realm of ideas that must become visible before they can produce any results. How? Through illustration and design. (When was the last time you saw a piece of typewritten copy run as an ad?) That great idea that's in your head requires visual form before it becomes an ad.

Don't become discouraged because your drawing skill might stop at stick figures. Nobody expects you to be Leonardo da Vinci. What *is* required is a reasonable sense of the space you have available to you and a clear understanding of the priority of the elements you are preparing. In other words, you know the "weight" to assign to the elements and your rudimentary layout should indicate this. (You may even hear the term "rough rough" used for this step, which reflects its very preliminary nature.)

In the beginning, you may find yourself thinking of words with little regard for the final design of the finished ad. One thing at a time, you tell yourself. First, let me get the words down and then I'll worry about the layout. While this is perfectly normal for the beginner, you'll discover it's less than satisfactory as your skills improve.

Before long, you'll start thinking of words and pictures in tandem. You'll start designing the layout in your head even as you scribble the words on paper. You might even think of the graphic idea *before* you set down a single word! The point is, you must eventually learn to "see" your ad as you write it. Even if the final design turns out quite differently (and probably much improved!) from the way you visualized it at the outset.

Right now, "design" is probably not your strong suit. It might even scare you a little, but it shouldn't. We simply want to point out its importance to a copywriter. As you progress, you'll gradually pick up enough of a sense of design to fill your needs. And don't be surprised if you find out you have more talent in this area than you ever dreamed. After all, to be a copywriter is to be an idea person. Up to now, you've simply been confining your ideas to the written word. Now you've been unchained; you no longer have such limitations!

Eyeflow

Imagine a blank sheet of paper. As you start to assemble words and pictures on this page, you do so in a carefully consid-

How many ways to Layout an Ad?
Add a few yourself—

Try putting STORE NAME at the top of your ad -- or what else? <u>Same</u> ad, <u>same</u> copy

LAYOUT DESIGN: With a little ingenuity, the same elements can be arranged in many different ways.

ered sequence: this is the order that you believe is most logical and most persuasive to your cause.

The trick is to get the reader to follow in your footsteps. That's why "eyeflow" is paramount in the structure of your ad. You want to capture your readers' eyes and then lead them, step by step, along the path you have planned. You don't want them to jump around because then they might lose track of the message. Worse, their eyes might glide right out of the ad, and the page gets turned.

If the headline ends at the far right side of the page, don't have the subhead (which you presumably want read next) at the far left. Chances are, the reader won't bother glancing back there. Don't have copy set so wide that readers end up playing an eyeball tennis game. They won't; they'll tire and be gone. Don't expect readers to come to the end of a section of text and then jump high up and over an illustration to get the rest of it. It's hard enough to grab readers. When you do, don't make it hard for them to stick with you.

The same goes for the illustration. When possible, have it "point" to the element you want read next. For example, the arrangement of the subject or the product in the illustration could narrow at one point, directing your eye in the right direction. Photos or artwork in silhouette or vignette can easily be designed to direct attention in a certain way. The subject in the illustration can also help by being posed to look in the chosen direction. It's worth noting here that you should always avoid having your subject look out of the ad because readers have been shown to follow their gaze—right out of the ad. Models should be photographed facing toward the action, not away from it.

Make it easy for readers. Determine the order in which you want your ad viewed and then work closely with your art director to make sure it happens that way. Don't give the eye any alternative but the direction you decide.

Occasionally, your discipline in this area will be challenged. Someone will say, "Don't worry about eyeflow. The ad looks so much better this way." Beware! An ad might *look* great yet fail to guide readers in the right direction, so that they slip away before the message is registered. Follow the fundamentals. The eyeflow test is one that every layout should pass before you proceed any further.

But clearly this is not the case. Open any magazine and pick out those ads that never took this test: you'll see "fences" that block readership rather than the "eye highways" that make it easy for your eyes to glide from start to finish, just the way the copywriter planned it.

Balance

An ad is not like a seesaw, calling for perfectly equal weight on both sides, balanced on some invisible center point. This kind of symmetry is perfectly correct, of course. But you are not bound by it and indeed, if all ads were so uniformly structured it would cause a dreary sameness that would prevent advertising from achieving its first goal: Get seen!

Still, balance is important; its definition is simply less rigid than you might expect. The main thing to remember is not to let your layout get too heavy on one side or the other, or on top. As the layout develops, keep these considerations in mind. But also remember that different type faces (bold or light), sizes (large or small) and settings (loose or tight) have different weights in a layout. Likewise the illustration: a photograph is generally "heavier" than line art.

Even though the layout itself might seem to strike a good balance, this might not hold when the actual type and illustration are finally in place. Make sure you and your art director consider the appearance of the *finished* elements before you are satisfied the layout is balanced.

On p. 109 you'll see some very simple examples of how balance can be achieved without symmetry. Try starting with your Headline or Text area (one or both) flush left or flush right and see what happens. Then follow this procedure routinely from now on.

Dominance

Every element can't possibly have equal importance in an ad; something must be dominant. Why? Because otherwise a reader isn't given reason to stop and doesn't know where to start. The dominant element could be the Headline, or the Illustration—or even the Logo. (In cigarette advertising, for instance,

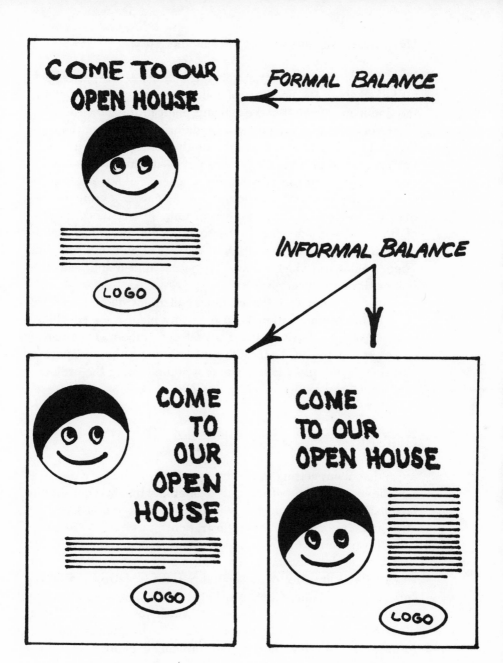

FORMAL BALANCE

INFORMAL BALANCE

COME TO OUR OPEN HOUSE

LOGO

COME TO OUR OPEN HOUSE

LOGO

COME TO OUR OPEN HOUSE

LOGO

using flush right hed

using flush left hed

AN EXERCISE IN BALANCE: Here you see the headline centered, flush right and flush left. The visual "weight" of the elements is an important factor in such balance.

the name of the brand often gets top billing.) A few pages back we talked about the necessity of controlling the reader's eyeflow; the dominant element is the starting point in this process.

Every problem you face will be different. One time the solution will be a striking photograph. Another time, a powerful headline promise. Another time, just the price—if that's the most compelling appeal you can make (it often is in retail advertising).

You may even, on occasion, choose to cluster a group of elements to form one dominant visual unit. For instance, photos of three dress models might be so grouped. But when this is done, make sure they're not all of equal size and in a row, but "stepped down," which adds to the visual appeal and leads the reader through the ad.

Bear in mind that the dominant element doesn't have to "shout" in the conventional sense. A tiny picture (or Headline) in a sea of white space can be a real eye-grabber. Dominance comes as much from being different and doing the unexpected as it does from simply taking the easy route—doing the ordinary in a bigger and louder way.

CLIP ART

What about getting some illustrations for an ad for a newspaper client or a local retail account—something that fits your simple layouts? The production staff will help you pick and fit the type style and size, but how about illustrations?

Clip art comes to your rescue on a newspaper. Huge volumes of it are normally available. The two most popular publishers of this material are Metro Associated Services (Metro) and SCW, Inc. (formerly Stamps-Conhaim). Subscribers to these services are welcome to use the copyrighted art, which you can just clip out of the clip books and paste on your layout. Each volume is indexed for faster reference and each month usually contains art for holidays occurring that month for easier advertising tie-ins.

If your newspaper is printed by offset, which many now are, be very careful with your clip art because it will actually be photographed from your layout when it reaches production. Make no pencil marks on it. Each piece of clip art has a number, and it is good practice to jot that number on the outside margin of

adidas RUNNING SHOES

AC 1175 Country
Special padding for protection of heel and Achilles tendon. Arch support extra-thick heel wedge.

AC 1917 Country Girl
Made on narrower ladies last, white with green stripes.

3465 Runner
Top-rated running shoe with mesh nylon uppers, velour reinforced. Durable star profile sole.

3467 Lady Runner
Made on narrower ladies last, light blue with white stripes.

adidas TRACK/FIELD SHOES

5118 Apollo
A shoe for natural tracks. Extra padding underneath heel for comfortable run. Six interchangeable spikes and antimicrobial inlay sole.

5112 Jet
Uppers of rugged blue nylon. Soft ankle collar padding. Cushiony heel for extra protection.

5110 Apollo
Nylon upper. Outside toe, heel counter. Padded tongue. Flexible foot-form nylon sole. Screw-in spike system. 4 spikes.

5107 Interval II
Nylon uppers with velour reinforcement. Oxford cut. Extensive padding. Nylon sole.

YOUR PUBLICATION HAS THE KWIKEE SYSTEM
Simply cut out illustration and paste on layout.
©1979 Multi-Ad Services, Inc.   Peoria, Illinois 61652

'80 K3D-B108

CLIP ART FROM MANUFACTURER: Many companies provide their customers with this type of artwork for use in assembling retail ads for individual stores. By also providing brief copy, they help make sure product descriptions are correct. *Courtesy Adidas USA Inc.*

your ad layout sheet so you can easily find the art again in a duplicate clip art book if it is lost while going through production.

You also will have to jot the number of the clip art on the outside margin of your ad if your newspaper is still being reproduced by hot type. (You will know this the first day you're on the job.) One caution about using clip art that usually helps beginning copywriters: don't waste time trimming neatly around it. Remember what *is white* is going to photograph and reproduce *as white*. So just cut it out and keep going! Do treat clip books with care, however, because they usually are also used by other staff members.

Of course, clip art is not the only source for illustrations. Many manufacturers supply their retailers with product art in the form of photographs, clip books and even fully completed ads (admats, slicks, repro-proofs) that merely require the insertion of the retailer's name, address and telephone number, along with any appropriate price information. Furthermore, many newspapers are adding artists to their staffs—good news for harried copywriters!

The volume of words written for print advertising far surpasses those written for any other medium. Because you will use words so often, it is important for you to have a grasp of the fundamentals presented in this chapter. From this point you will be able to proceed to the special skills needed for each specific medium in the print category.

Copywriting for different print media

7

There are a number of different print media that you're familiar with and for which you'll be writing advertising. The guidelines noted in the previous chapter are, of course, applicable throughout, even though they may need to be modified for the specific medium being used. Outdoor billboards and direct mail will clearly have different requirements even though the general rules remain the same. This chapter will concentrate on ways to take maximum advantage of the different opportunities offered by several different print media.

NEWSPAPERS

Newspapers get the major portion of the total dollars spent each year for advertising. To readers, newspapers are very urgent; they mean action. Now. Today and tomorrow. Not next week or next month.

Newspaper ads are full of news—usually "sales" of one kind

AD COPY

The headline, together with the illustration, is the most important element in an ad . . . if it's a sound one. The headline should not merely repeat the message conveyed by the art — it should add strength to the illustration and stop the reader — by offering a benefit, stating news, demanding action or simply startling the reader to attention.

Stopping the reader is, of course, not enough. You must hold his or her attention long enough to put across your sales message. Remember that few people read every word in a newspaper — and your ad is vying for attention against world news, notes on the folks next door, comic strips and other ads! "Talk" to the reader in a friendly, enthusiastic manner — give him all the facts he wants to know about what you have for sale. Never sacrifice information just to be clever and don't use large or tricky words. Keep it simple, direct, warm in tone — and FACTUAL.

CHECK YOUR COPY
for THE FOLLOWING:

1. Does the headline stop the reader and strengthen the illustration?

2. Does the sub-head and/or body copy follow the headline logically, maintaining the reader's interest?

3. Have all the facts on sizes, colors, kinds of materials, etc., been included?

4. Has a reason for immediate action by the reader been given?

5. Has the reader been invited to immediate action?

6. Is the name of the store, the address, telephone and other pertinent information included?

7. Is the copy written and displayed in relationship to the size of the ad and the illustration?

HELPFUL HINTS: This handy checklist is something you'll want to consult often. *Courtesy SCW, Inc.*

or another. But how can you make your "sale" even newsier and therefore worth more attention? The idea is to find its benefit to shoppers and to shout it loudly and clearly. "What's in it for me?" is the unspoken question every reader asks and that every good ad must answer. (See Chapter 4.) If your sale offers something exclusive, say so. If you have a bigger selection, say so. If your sale offers an unexpected bonus (free alterations, immediate delivery), say so. Price is invariably the star of most local retail advertising, but to neglect these other advantages that might make your sale different and more attractive to shoppers is a big mistake.

Another point to remember: people read ads from the top down. So give top billing to the selling message. Don't waste that space with the store name. At least don't *automatically* include the store name in the headline. Readers will find the store name just as easily if it's down at the bottom, where they expect it. The idea is to give readers your strongest selling story at the start, before they turn the page.

The copywriter who writes copy for a supermarket, major discount chain or drug store must work with a different format, called an "omnibus" ad, which is a grab bag of various products and prices; the store itself is the main attraction.

The major difference in what has been said previously about format is that now you will be thinking in terms of writing copy to fill a series of small areas. Although you type a Copy Sheet as usual, your keying becomes crucial; there can be absolutely no question where each piece of copy appears in the finished ad. (See pp. 116–117)

To make your job easier, you may want to work out an arrangement with your artist or production manager that whatever you type in capital letters should be set in headline-size type.

MAGAZINES

For most beginning copywriters magazine ads are the most difficult, the most demanding but the most enjoyable. While it would be rare that a new copywriter would be asked to write an ad for an $80,000 page in *Time* magazine, you could very well be expected to write ads that will appear in industrial or trade magazines. (Note: most people in the business refer to maga-

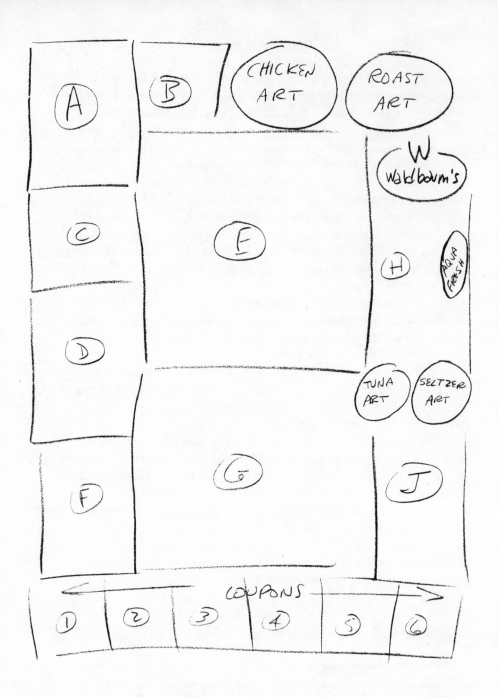

OMNIBUS LAYOUT: This very rough layout has its many elements clearly identified by key letters that refer to the typed copy on an accompanying Copy Sheet. There can be no mistaking exactly what goes where.

FINISHED OMNIBUS AD: With so many different elements, the need for a clearly keyed layout becomes apparent. The various art elements (meat, mushrooms, tuna cans) are often available from either the manufacturer of the product or a Clip Art service (see p. 111). *Courtesy Waldbaum Inc.*

zines as "books.") There's really no difference for a copywriter. You start with a USP and proceed from there. In consumer ads, the stakes are higher because the costs are higher, that's all.

Copywriting for magazines is different from writing ads for newspapers in one important respect. Your target spends more time with a magazine, and if it's a consumer magazine, readers look upon it as fun, leisure reading for two or three hours—or more. When writing consumer ads for consumer magazines try to weave a little sales story rather than using the "get in and get out quickly" newspaper approach. But this does not mean padding your ad.

Magazine ads can be described as having the three essential elements of a good story: an opening, a middle and a close. You always open with a big idea because that's the very best way to capture attention (and without that the rest of your efforts will be in vain). This should be based on your USP as explained previously: the strongest possible statement of your strongest competitive advantage. And remember, this doesn't have to be stated in the conventional manner either. Occasionally it can be provocative (remember the famous Volkswagen "Lemon" ad?) or unexpected ("We're only Number 2" was a surprising theme for Avis when it first appeared). Maybe graphics can be used to express the headline idea instead of words. Even though this will be the exception rather than the rule, it's well to know this technique is available to you. Any relevant way of attracting attention to the main message is legitimate.

So much for a good, strong opening. What goes in the middle? First, be sure you immediately back up your opening statement with solid features and benefits. They fill the middle. Beware of being cute. Also beware of trying to fool your readers. Starved for copy? Then you don't know enough about the product or your target, as discussed in Chapter 4. Another problem with the middle of a magazine ad is that your writing style may become choppy. Some solutions to this problem are suggested in Chapter 5.

Close your magazine ad with an attempt to wrap up the entire ad by a quick reference to what you said in the headline. Just restate it slightly in the close, along with, of course, a call to action.

You have just told a magazine advertising sales story to your

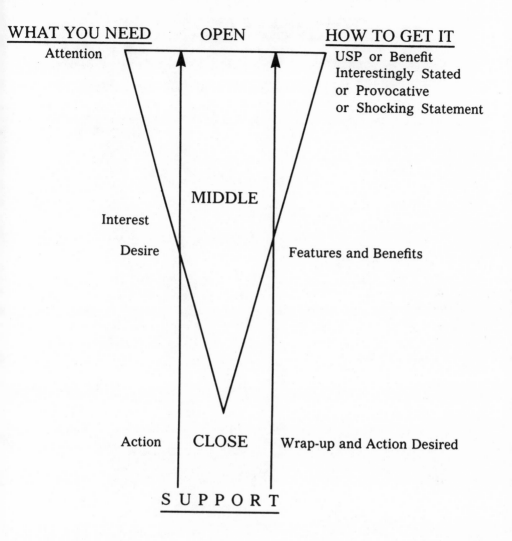

WHAT YOU NEED   OPEN   HOW TO GET IT

Attention

USP or Benefit
Interestingly Stated
or Provocative
or Shocking Statement

MIDDLE

Interest

Desire   Features and Benefits

Action   CLOSE   Wrap-up and Action Desired

S U P P O R T

STRUCTURE FOR WRITING MAGAZINE ADS: The discipline demonstrated in this chart stands as a guide for beginners and a reminder
for all others.

THE FIRST BOAT SHOE DESIGNED TO PERFORM AS WELL ON LAND AS IT DOES AT SEA.

The boat shoe we're referring to is made by Timberland.® And it's the first one that takes into account this simple fact:

MOST PEOPLE WHO WEAR BOAT SHOES NEVER SET FOOT ON A BOAT.

The boat shoe, as we know it today, is actually a misnomer.

Because what started out as something worn exclusively by people who sail is now something worn by virtually everyone.

Today, boat shoes are as acceptable with a sport jacket and tie on Saturday night as they are with foul-weather gear that same afternoon.

The problem is, while their acceptance has improved tremendously, the quality of boat shoes hasn't.

THE TIMBERLAND® BOAT SHOE VS. THE SPERRY TOP-SIDER.®

When people think of boat shoes, one name always comes to mind. Sperry Top-Sider.®

We're about to change that. And we've started at the bottom.

The sole on Sperry's biggest selling boat shoe is made of a rubber compound. Timberland's is a long-lasting, rugged Vibram® sole.

Theirs is anti-skid, anti-slip; excellent on boats. So is ours.

But where Sperry's biggest selling boat shoe falls down is on land. Sperry's sole is stitched directly to their uppers. When the stitching breaks, Sperry's sole flaps. Timberland's sole is bonded to a mid-sole. Ours won't flap.

But the heart of a Timberland boat shoe isn't just the sole. Like Sperry's biggest selling model, Timberland's uppers are made only of full-grain leathers. Unlike Sperry's, which have an applied pigment

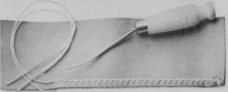

Timberland uses oil or silicone-impregnated leathers. They remain soft and supple for the life of the shoe. Sperry's biggest selling model has an applied pigment finish.

Our laces are thick rawhide. Our eyelets are solid brass. Sperry eyelets are painted aluminum, which can chip and peel.

An abrasion count measures a sole's resistance to abrasion, a good indication of durability. The higher the number, the better. Timberland's count is 140, more than any other leading manufacturer.*

finish, Timberland's are silicone or oil-impregnated. Ours look more natural and feel softer than theirs.

We use only solid brass eyelets. They use painted aluminum ones.

The result of using only the highest quality materials and Timberland's unmatched handsewn moccasin construction is a boat shoe so comfortable, the breaking-in period ends the day you put

them on.

So what it comes down to is this: You can get a pair of boat shoes designed to hold up well just on a boat. Or a pair of boat shoes designed to hold up.

Timberland ®

The Timberland Company,
P.O. Box 370, Newmarket, New Hampshire 03857

*NBS abrasion tests conducted according to ASTM standards. Actual wear you get out of Timberland boat shoes depends on individual usage.

A GOOD MAGAZINE AD, like a good story, has a beginning (Headline/ Benefit Statement), a middle (Text/Description of Advantages) and close (Logo/Product to Look For). Many sales points can be made, although all must support the main Headline. *Courtesy The Timberland Company.*

target who is sitting in an easy chair thinking about how to spend her or his next $20 to $200. Next, this same reader will be looking for the product (or a deal on it) at a local store. Open. Middle. Close. Just like any good salesperson.

DIRECT RESPONSE

This is a field that's growing by leaps and bounds. Why? It offers great convenience, especially in the soaring number of 2-worker families. It also cuts down on driving and gas consumption. And the quality of the merchandise gets better all the time. While direct *mail* remains the cornerstone, direct response has burgeoned to include magazines, television (especially cable television)—and even telephone! We will concentrate here on the mail and magazine segments because they are the biggest and offer the most opportunities for copywriters.

DIRECT MAIL

Very simply, this is represented by all those envelopes and packets that you receive because you're on some "mailing list." Since most of this is unsolicited, your first job is to get the envelope opened!

How you do this will depend on the product and the image you want to project. Sometimes a discreet envelope with a hand-affixed stamp is appropriate. Other times you might want to shout from every square inch of envelope space. Both have been shown to work.

The post office is fussy about keeping the address clear, so be sure to check with your local postmaster before you begin. While you're there, pick up any booklets about bulk mailing rates and postage-paid reply mailings.

In recent years there has been a trend to use what is normally the back side of the envelope (where the sealing flap is) for the stamp, address of the recipient and also the return address (which does not include a telephone number). This gives you an unbroken front surface on the envelope for your "teaser" or reason for opening it. Direct-mail users, who have bigger budgets, often use a see-through window on the envelope to allow a peek at the exciting contents inside even before the envelope is opened.

Among the nitty-gritty details to be solved when writing your direct mail is how it will be addressed: by hand, by pressure-sensitive labels or by machine? Obviously hand-addressing would be an almost impossible task for any large mailing. The importance of using a good mailing list was discussed in Chapter 3. Surely not all direct mail is in letter format, but it all must be addressed in some way.

If it's a letter, you'll have to decide rather quickly whether it will have a personalized address and salutation or no inside address and a generalized salutation (for example, "Dear Card-member"). Or should it just start with no inside address, no salutation but possibly a printed headline or typed lines in capital letters? And, of course, there are variations of all these ways that are worth considering. These are just starters.

Another early consideration when writing your direct-mail copy is the letterhead. Are you going to use the company's standard one or do you prefer to create a special one to fit your message or the occasion?

Who will sign the letter and how (if you've decided to use a letter format) are the next problems. Do you feel the letters should be signed personally (quite a chore), signed by machine, or signed on the master copy (if printing by offset)?

Having dispensed with these considerations, think about the body of the copy by following the suggestions in Chapter 4. Above all, remember that direct mail is costing you money in postage and preparation. Be sure, then, to include a strong action step, and make it easy to do. Don't expect people to sit down and write their own letters to you in reply. It's unrealistic in this busy world. Some direct-mail offers include a free gift just to get a reply. The least you should do is offer a toll-free telephone number to call or enclose a postage-paid reply card, which the U.S. Postal Service will be glad to help you design because it requires certain information to appear on your postage-paid reply card in a prescribed way, including the little lines along the right-hand side. They're not decoration; they're required. Likewise, you need a permit number for postage-paid replies. However, it's worth all the trouble because you're only paying for the replies you actually get.

BUSINESS REPLY MAIL
FIRST CLASS   PERMIT NO. 73026   WASHINGTON, DC

POSTAGE WILL BE PAID BY ADDRESSEE

**NO POSTAGE
NECESSARY
IF MAILED
IN THE
UNITED STATES**

Philatelic Sales Division
United States Postal Service
Washington, DC 20265

BUSINESS REPLY MAIL: This sample contains the mandatory information required by the U.S. Postal Service, which issues the appropriate
permit. The minimum size for such mail is 3½" × 5". If your assignment
is to update an existing envelope or card, simply paste it on a large
sheet of paper and make the appropriate revisions. There is no need
for a new visual sheet unless the design is changing. *Courtesy United
States Postal Service.*

Using gimmicks

To increase the chance that your message gets attention and
is read, you might consider using a gimmick or gadget on the
letter. Let's face it: the average person is bombarded by such
mail, both at home and at business. Some people even resent
it. It becomes your task to make it as inviting as possible. Who,
for instance, could resist reading the letter if there's a small plastic
watering can glued (tipped) on it? Maybe it's a letter from a seed
house offering 12 packages of assorted flower seeds for $4. Maybe
it's from a bank offering to show you how to make your savings
grow! Regardless, you've made your mailing piece a little different, and its chances of being read increase. These flat, plastic
gadgets come in hundreds of designs—hammers, umbrellas,
hearts, automobiles, airplanes, you name it.

One company did a mailing using a regular teabag. Another company mailed a full-length, plastic drinking straw. Choose whatever your imagination dictates as long as the gadget has a direct relationship to the message and is mentioned in the letter. Even commemorative U.S. postage stamps have had a corner lightly glued on a letter, and who's not going to stop at least long enough to remove something like this?

Besides being sure the gadget has a relationship to your message, make certain that it will not break when mailed. For example, one company used an interesting plastic whistle, which unfortunately was not flat. It arrived in pieces—not the most welcome thing to fall all over a desk or living room rug. When considering gadgets, be sure to avoid flammable materials or anything that could possibly be dangerous. One razor blade manufacturer distributed free blades with disastrous effects when some accidentally found their way into children's hands.

Multiple mailings

An effective mail order technique uses a sequence of mailings to the same recipients. For instance, one magazine accomplishes this by sending the usual cautionary letter when a subscription is about to expire. If the subscriber ignores this warning, a few weeks later the magazine dramatically sends an empty mailing wrapper with a message saying how sorry it is about not being able to send the magazine. If the subscriber still refuses to respond, next comes the subscriber's actual mailing plate along with a final plea for renewal. The old 1-2-3 punch!

Another variation of this follow-up idea is used by a company seeking to "soften up" a dealer or a purchasing agent for the manufacturer's sales representative. Each week for several weeks the target receives a single part of some game or other device. The device is still incomplete when, during the last week, in walks the representative with the missing piece that finishes the unit. He's usually welcome! Such imaginative use of multiple mailings can be very effective.

Building store traffic

Some manufacturers use direct mail to help increase traffic at their local dealers by "remote control." It works this way: your mailing goes to your best potential customers with a validation card in it. When the potential customer goes to the dealership to see the particular product mentioned in the mailing, the dealer stamps the card. The potential customer mails the card back to the manufacturer and in return gets a free gift directly from the company. This is not inexpensive, but it can get good results if the product involved is well chosen.

Some warnings

Watch the weight and size of your direct mailing. You don't want to spend double the usual postage, nor do you want to buy special-size envelopes. Plan to use standard-size envelopes. And if it's a big mailing, management shouldn't plan to do it with its own regular secretarial staff. It will most probably bottle up the main office for a week! The Yellow Pages lists professional direct-mail houses that will be glad to help with all these chores, which includes getting the mailing out on time.

If your budget is too limited to add some color here and there for a word, phrase or underline, why not use colored paper stock? And even if your have no selection of type, your own typewriter (or your secretary's) can type an interesting master copy for offset printing by using just typewriter characters. You can underline, use capital letters, space more or less between lines or paragraphs, add extra space between letters or words, or step capitalized words down (if not overdone). But normally you should try to do something that at least gives the letter an interesting appearance. Your competition is fierce.

MAGAZINE MAIL ORDER

Magazine mail-order advertising poses a stiff challenge for a copywriter. The ad you write—whether it's full-page size or a tiny ⅙ page—represents the sole point of contact between buyer and seller. You're not asking a person to go to a store where the product can be seen and tried—and then accepted or rejected. You're asking a reader to believe your promise, to trust your product, and then to purchase it sight unseen. That's a tall order. That's why mail-order ads are straightforward rather than fancy. They realize this is the only shot they've got at that prospect.

These ads brim with "reason why" copy. They normally offer the opportunity to pay via credit card, which is easy for most people. Some even provide an 800 telephone number to make it easy to make the purchase. A mail order copywriter can make things happen!

Coupons

Magazines are often used for mail-order sales by including coupons in the ad. Some will also give you a "plug" (free publicity) in the editorial columns when you advertise in their publication— if you're smart enough to ask for it. Success will often depend not only on picking an interesting mail-order item (which is normally out of the copywriter's control) but also on how easy you make purchasing. That can mean, among other things, the size of the coupon. When space is tight, try making the entire mail-order ad a coupon to be torn out and mailed. Leave plenty of space for name and address. Otherwise, you may discourage the reader from taking action, or this information will be hard to read and lead to improperly filled orders. As difficult as it may seem, you still need to consider the material discussed in the design section of Chapter 6. A dominant element in mail-order advertising in a magazine or newspaper is critical. Everything cannot be equally important in small space because then nothing is important!

Normally the wording on the coupon the reader will tear out and return is very personal. Your name and address should be on the coupon itself because often it's torn out to be filled in later. The text area can include such phrases as; "Yes, rush me your booklet about . . ." A coupon can be handled easily on your Copy Sheet by adding the element Coupon and treating it as one piece of copy with one key (see the omnibus ad format discussion in this chapter). You may want to use some capital letters in the body of the coupon or work closely with your artist, who will try to give it some distinctive treatment. Be sure you include all the details on your coupon that the factory will need to fill the order.

Split runs

"Split run" refers to a publisher's ability to "split" the printing of a given issue of his newspaper or magazine, with half going

With 12 pages of pants in our 64-page catalog, you know we've made a commitment.

(We'd better be right)

A commitment to quality at the high end:

Witness these beautiful Sea Island cotton dress trousers. There simply are no finer threads woven into cloth than these, spun from the coastal cotton of Georgia and the Carolinas. Nor does the impeccable tailoring favor men over women. These are cut to fit either, as quality trousers should. Soft, silky, almost weightless. In Tan, and only $48.

A commitment to quality at a rock-bottom price:

We doubt if $15 ever bought a better-made pair of trousers than our poplin "Coolers," available in Tan, Navy and a bright Breton Red for both men and women. If they weren't a solid value we wouldn't offer them. You certainly don't need another source of trousers that are merely inexpensive.

This by no means exhausts the commitment we've made, now that we've decided Lands' End will be a leader in the trouser business.

Our catalog features 100% cotton casual pants—colorful rugby and "painter's" pants, drawstring pants, and familiar "putter" pants made by Stubbies, our Australian short-shorts manufacturer.

Check out our full range of quality twills, those tough yet correct trousers pioneered by the military, priced from $17.50 to $39. Or our tropical worsted trousers at $39, guaranteed the best you can buy at that price or your money back.

More pants than space!

And more. Dress poplins for men and women. Pure cotton seersuckers. Stretch jeans, and dressier stretch trousers you can wear to the office. Cargo jeans. And more slacks, shorts and swim trunks of all kinds than we have space to mention.

Quality comes first with us in all our merchandise, from trousers to soft luggage. Only then do we ask price to come to terms with it. Never the other way around.

If we're new to you, we don't ask that you trust us. Simply try us, by calling toll-free 24 hours a day at 800-356-4444 (Wisconsin call 608-935-2788). Or fill out the coupon and let us mail you a free copy of our catalog.

☐ **Please send free 64-page catalog.**

Lands' End Dept. A-03
Dodgeville, WI 53533

Name _____

Address _____

City _____

State _____ Zip _____

Or call Toll-free:

800-356-4444

(Except Wisconsin call 608-935-2788).

LANDS' END
DIRECT MERCHANTS

of fine wool and cotton sweaters, Oxford buttondown shirts, snow wear, deck wear, original Lands' End soft luggage and a multitude of other quality goods from around the world.

MAIL ORDER ADS sell hard from start to finish. They brim with facts, including price, because they must make their case and close the deal before you turn the page. *Courtesy Land's End.*

to one group of subscribers and half to the other. It offers an advertiser an opportunity to run one version of an ad in half the copies and another version in the other half of the copies. Each coupon will be given a special key code to tell them apart. Then you can sit back and see which ad pulls best.

It's most common to test two different prices in this way. You might be surprised to know that it's not always the lowest price that gets the best response! But you should also consider this an opportunity to test different USPs as well. If you're selling cheese, for example, you might want to test an appetite appeal against a "perfect gift" appeal. Or a luggage maker could try a "long life" appeal vs. a purely prestige appeal. A split run gives you this chance. Since the audience demographics, the timing, and everything else are identical for both versions, the only variable is the price or the appeal. Once you know which works best, you'll have the direction for the remainder of your advertising campaign.

One warning: make sure the publication has no plans to run a coupon (for another product) on the reverse side of yours because it will reduce your response.

OUTDOOR

According to the Outdoor Advertising Association of America, Inc., the following are some creative guidelines to consider when planning and writing your copy for this medium. In outdoor, the word "copy" is taken to mean the entire advertisement including illustrations and text. And in outdoor the importance of copy cannot be overstated. The difference in readership and remembrance between a well-designed poster and a poor one can well be 50% or greater. Obviously, the space cost is the same.

When creating copy for outdoor, two unique characteristics of the medium must be kept in mind: it communicates with people on the move and at a distance. Therefore, outdoor advertising must be simple, arresting and legible. It has only a brief period in which to be seen and to register its message. Economy of ideas, elements and words is paramount. All nonessentials must be eliminated (see pp. 46–47). A maximum of seven "takes" (words or pictures) is a good guideline for outdoor brevity.

Good copy starts with a single idea, proceeds with an original expression of that idea, and concludes with the execution in the simplest, most dramatic, most easily visible terms. Each element should do its own job so that words, pictures and layout contribute without overlapping. Lettering should be clear, simple and bold.

How can you visualize what your outdoor sign will look like to your fast-moving audience? Outdoor advertising companies (organizations that rent billboards) will give you a viewing device that lets you simulate the way your poster will look to a passing driver. Use it. You may be surprised at what you see!

Just remember that different media have different characteristics and different audience compositions. This will determine the way you write your message and the way you frame your appeal.

Copywriting for broadcast media

8

From a writer's viewpoint, radio and television are quite a bit different from newspapers and magazines. For one thing, there's the matter of time. In print, there's no limit to the amount of time readers can spend with your ad. If they're particularly interested, your ad will be read and reread to make sure it's understood. Or a retail ad will be pored over carefully by a shopper with an eye for bargains. Or your coupon will be clipped. The attention span of your ad is unlimited, and while you can't always count on capturing a reader's fancy for any great length, the possibility exists and it's a factor to consider in the way you present your message.

The broadcast media, on the other hand, offer no such luxury for you. Time is tightly controlled. Your spot will be 60 seconds or 30 seconds or 10 seconds. Exactly. Not one second more. Yet within that rigid framework you should follow the same formula that works for print advertising: Attention, Interest, Desire, Action (AIDA). Of course, the rules of the game and the tools you have to work with must be adjusted when you shift gears and move into broadcast.

RADIO

When you write for radio, you write for the ear. Ideally, you'll create images that listeners see in their minds' eyes. But the only way to attain this vision is through the ear. You have three tools to work with—words, music and sound effects.

Rarely does your target audience deliberately sit down to listen to the radio, which immediately makes your job different and more difficult. Radio listeners are normally half tuned out even when they (and you) think they're tuned in! Radio is essentially a passive medium. It's usually somewhere in the background "noise" in the house, in the car or at the office. Your first big task, then, is (once again) to get your listener's attention. Are you going to try to get it with sound effects, music or the announcer's voice?

To avoid just entertaining the world at your client's expense, when writing your radio spot be sure that in a 60-second spot you identify your client at least three times by name (usually at the start, in the middle and at the end) and give the address at least twice. For a 30-second commercial, include both the client's name and address at least twice. In a 10-second spot, at least once for each.

As a rule of thumb, you can calculate that in a 60-second commercial you will have about 150–160 spoken words. A 30-second spot has 75–80 words. A 10-second spot contains about 30 words. Any sound effects or music will subtract, naturally, from your total word count, unless it's just in the background with the announcer talking over it.

"Think time" is an important asset when you're writing radio commercials. Look at the clock and think how long you're allowing the introductory music to play (if there is any). Too long? Too short? Think about it while you watch the clock and you'll soon get a "think time" sense in your writing.

You're already familiar with the use of words in print advertising. In radio, they're just as important—maybe more so! Just keep the following points in mind:

• Don't use ten-dollar words. Keep them simple. Your listeners don't have the chance to ponder your meaning or to go back and think it over.

- Avoid hard-to-pronounce words. Remember that the letter "p" has a tendency to "pop" and the letter "s" often sounds like a hiss over the airways.

- Watch out for words like "we" and "our." To the listener, does "we" refer to the advertiser or the station? But freely use "you" and "your" since there can be no mistake in their meaning.

- Use contractions when possible. Write the way people talk. Radio is very personal.

- Don't overload your commercial. One idea is enough. Don't try to cram in too much because nothing will be remembered.

When you think your radio script is ready, read it *aloud* and time it. Can you say all the words? Any hesitation? Any stumbling? Is there breathing space? If you have a hard time with it, so will the announcer.

Music

Music is a whole new element that you can mix into your radio copy. But don't let it scare you. You don't have to be a professional musician to make good use of music. Most radio stations have music libraries that you can use to find music to use with your commercial. If you're recording your spot in a studio, you'll undoubtedly find the studio has its own music library or has access to one. Or you'll be directed to a "music house"—a specialty company that has a library of many thousands of titles and numerous arrangements of each. They also have skilled people to help you find what you want. Just describe it as best you can: "gay circus music" written on your script would be enough to get you several tunes that meet that description. All this is done for a fee, of course. Advertising agencies make extensive use of this type of facility. But even small retailers should know that this source of music is available—if they're not able to get free production help from their local radio station.

Creating original music is something else. It invariably starts with the words—and that means you! Once again, as a writer you aren't expected to create the music—that's a job for specialists. Advertising agencies work with many of these professionals in most major cities. Recording studios and radio stations can also help you find someone to aid you in this situation. While many people do this full time, there's also much free-lance talent available in this field.

A couple of warnings about using original music are in order. You'll be dealing with unions, in most cases, and that means strict regulations. You don't pay musicians a flat fee for their services; the pay scale is based on "residuals," which means the more the music is used, the more the musicians get paid. You have to try to figure this into the final cost. Another thing: the more musicians, the more expensive it is. So if you can get by with a piano alone, it will be cheaper than a piano and five other pieces—and much cheaper when you start toting up possible residual payments! You should also know that if the same musician plays more than one instrument in the arrangement (done by overdubbing), he or she gets paid separately for each instrument. There are no bargains when you're recording original music!

Sound effects

Sound effects (SFX) are to radio commercials what pictures are to print advertising. (Music, of course, is also a sound effect, but it has already been discussed separately.) Sound effects play a big part in creating those mental images that are so vital for effective radio selling. And just as there's no limit to the type or style of illustrative material, there's virtually no limit to the kind of sound effects that are available. At one time these effects were done "live" by a specialist with a trunkful of tricks: he tinkled tea cups, slammed miniature doors or crinkled cellophane (which sounds like crackling fire) on cue. Now, more often than not, the sound you want is already on record or tape. Where? Once again, recording studios and radio stations have tapes of most basic sound effects right at their fingertips. What sound do you hear when you write the commercial? Write it down—you've got it.

Format

The format for a radio spot on a piece of paper will vary slightly depending upon where you're working. Every employer has his own little idiosyncrasies. However, basic formats are shown in the samples on pp. 135–136. Once again, as in print media, you are just beginning the life cycle of the advertisement. Your format should clearly communicate to the production staff what you want, which they can easily follow. Your script must line up, be underlined, and capitalized when necessary, as shown in the example.

Start your radio spot toward the top of the paper. There is no paragraphing, but other normal punctuation is used, including periods or dashes to indicate pauses (as long as it's not overdone). Phone numbers, when needed, should be repeated twice; if you want the number remembered, give your listeners a chance to write it down. This is particularly true for stores specializing in phone-in orders.

Avoid hyphenating words at the end of a line. Abbreviations are out except for A.M., P.M., Mr. or Mrs. Telephone numbers are always written numerically. But other numbers are written the way you want them pronounced: 1501 North Main Street is Fifteen-O-One North Main Street.

To have the announcer emphasize something in your script, just underline it or capitalize the word or words. Don't be guilty of writing a script for a lazy announcer. Make her or him work. Use the voice inflection for emphasis or for other reasons. When using more than one announcer in your commercial, you can give them names to make their identification easier for the production staff. An announcer needs clean copy; copy correction marks are not used.

Be sure you also include in your script instructions for handling the music. Some of the more familiar instructions are UP TO ESTABLISH (opening with music at full, normal sound level), GOES UNDER (barely heard in background as announcer speaks), UP AND OUT (music returns to full volume to end of spot).

Recording radio spots

As a copywriter, you'll usually be on hand when your radio commercial is recorded to make sure it turns out the way you intended (and in case any rewriting is needed). The talent will be assembled in a sound studio and after a brief rehearsal, the taping will begin. Don't be surprised if dozens of "takes" are required before it's done to everyone's satisfaction. If sound effects

Division of
J. Walter Thompson
Company

420 Lexington Avenue
New York, NY 10017
212 867 8300

Advertising Copy

Client	Date
CUNA	March 17, 1981

Job No	Unit
710707	:60 Radio

Subject	Draft No
Total Service	As recorded

(MUSIC THROUGHOUT)

HUSBAND: Honey, about our money problems...

WIFE: You mean our lack of liquid assets?

HUSBAND: Whatever. How'd it happen?

WIFE: The problem's domestic mismanagement. Look, Honey, our credit union could give us a better deal on almost everything the bank has. Like payroll deductions, so we can save a little each week -- painlessly, with good interest.

HUSBAND: I thought saving gave you hives.

WIFE: (laugh) Used to. But now that I'm working in the real world, we've gotta protect our interests. Oh, and then there are share drafts.

HUSBAND: Share drafts?

WIFE: They work like checks, but earn interest.

HUSBAND: Y'mean we'd get _paid_ instead of _charged_?

WIFE: Right. And credit unions usually give lower-interest loans than banks. Plus VISA cards, traveller's cheques, 24-hour automated tellers...

HUSBAND: And direct deposits for our paychecks -- so nothing happens to them.

WIFE: Like when you puréed your paycheck in the food processor, huh?

HUSBAND: At least I'm creative when it's my turn in the kitchen.

WIFE: Listen, Picasso, if the credit union's got all those things -- let's go!

HUSBAND: Okay!...Oh, but...can't right now....

WIFE: Why not?

HUSBAND: Well, I've, uh...got a souffle in the oven.

(MUSIC WITH VOCALS)

RECORDED RADIO SCRIPT: Note the use of sound effects (SFX) and such directions as (laugh). The copywriter must "hear" the commercial as it's being written. *Courtesy Credit Unions of North America.*

SELCHOW & RIGHTER COMPANY
SCRABBLE ® BRAND
60-SECOND RADIO

ANNCR: By now, you've probably made your list and
checked it twice. But if you're like most
Christmas shoppers, there's always "one more
thing" to buy. And we'd like to make a
suggestion: Scrabble ® Brand Crossword Game
from Selchow & Righter. That's right, Scrabble ®
Brand. It's almost a national institution. A
game that's fun for everyone, young and old, and
a game that gets played again and again. More
fun every time, too. Maybe that's why Scrabble ®
is now America's best-selling trademarked board
game. If you enjoy playing Scrabble ® . . .
and more people do every year . . . wouldn't
you like someone else to enjoy it too? You
can choose the Standard edition or the Deluxe
version that features a non-slip playing surface
on a turntable base. Scrabble ® Brand. The
All American word game. For anyone on your list.

(DEALER TAG)

LIVE RADIO SCRIPT: Because a commercial of this kind is read "live"
on the air by a staff announcer, it does not make use of sound effects
or music. On the other hand, it can often be personalized by adding a
reference to a local dealer at the end. *Courtesy Selchow & Righter Co.*

or music are required, they may or may not be included in this taping session. In any event, a "mix" must take place afterward, when all the voice, music, and effect tracks are merged into one.

Often, though, scripts alone are sent to the stations to be read by a staff announcer, sometimes live. This is less expensive, of course, since there are no costs for the announcer, music, or effects. It's also faster: what's written today can literally be on the air tomorrow in distant cities, transmitted by Telex. This comes in handy when a manufacturer wants to change prices fast or to keep a trade secret away from the competition until it's on the air. However, by letting a staff announcer read your script, you relinquish a certain amount of control: it may not come out the way you want and then it's too late. You're trading economy and speed for control. Sometimes it's a hard choice.

Some radio commercials are broadcast both recorded and live. How? When you want to include a local "dealer tag" at the end of the manufacturer's spot, rather than recording the name of each dealer (there could be hundreds!) and then let the individual stations pick the correct ones, it's far easier to leave 10 seconds at the end of the recorded spot where a live announcer can mention the local store name.

TELEVISION

Sight, sound, and motion come crashing together in the powerful medium of television. It's up to you to harness all this power for your message. Whatever you did for radio and print now joins forces with motion, demonstrations—action! You're not only involved with sound, music, announcer, actors—now you've got a cameraman and crew to contend with. This is show business!

One of the hardest jobs when writing for television is getting ideas and action on paper so you can communicate with the production staff. You'll need a script and a storyboard. The script defines the action; the storyboard is a visual portrayal of the action to be seen in the final commercial production. To write a TV commercial, you'll have to develop a feel for possible camera shots and know the technical terms to describe what you want. You'll find some of these terms listed on pages 138–141.

Just as in radio, TV again pits you against the clock: most

commercials run 10, 30 or 60 seconds in length. However, it's unreal to try to give you any word-count guidelines due to all the action that is possible and the visual elements that must be considered. For example, you could have a 30-second TV spot that's 20 seconds of visuals (video) before you hear a word spoken (audio).

Show and sell

Of all the reasons to use TV, one big one is for "show and tell." Better yet, "show and *sell*." Show by motion and demonstrations. This is what you can't do in print or radio. Use this to your client's maximum advantage. If you can communicate one good selling point in one TV commercial, you've done a good job. Don't try to overcrowd it with more than one major point.

Even more than when writing radio spots, in TV you must avoid entertaining the world at the expense of the client who's paying the bill. Strive to leave a memorable message about your client when the commercial is over. Television is a very personal medium; you're a guest in the viewer's room. Be friendly. Use contractions. Use "you" and "your." Be real. Be natural. Write like people talk.

SCRIPT DIRECTIONS
Camera Positions
When referring to people:

Head shot	Shoulders and head
Bust Shot	Center chest, shoulders and head
Waist Shot	Waist, center chest, etc.
Knee Shot	Knee, etc. (cut just above knee)
Full Shot	Entire person
Long Shot	Shown from a distance

For objects or groups of people:

CU—Close-up

Narrow-angle picture limited to object or part of one object instead of a scene. No background at all.

ECU—Extra Close-up

Very narrow angle, usually just one feature of an object or subject so that it completely fills the frame.

MCU—Medium Close-up

Medium-angle picture showing object and limited amount of background or setting.

MS—Medium shot

Wide angle showing objects and related material.

LS—Long Shot

Or establishing shot, full view in which figures or objects are smaller than frame and sensation of distance is achieved.

CAMERA MOVEMENTS

Pan

Scenes photographed by camera in fixed position but moved in a horizontal or vertical plane, usually following a moving subject.

Zoom

Shot obtained with a zoomar lens causing the scene, object, or title to increase or decrease in size (at any speed) without physically moving the camera. Differs from a dolly shot. A dolly shot changes perspective and relationship of objects. A zoom shot changes size of objects but maintains same perspective.

Dolly

Scenes photographed as camera moves either to or from subject. Gets its name from wheeled mount used for camera and operator.

Whip

A type of panning shot in which the camera is swung very rapidly on its vertical axis producing a blurred sensation when viewed; also known as a swish or zip pan.

OTHER USEFUL TERMS

Cut

Change from one scene to another.

Dissolve

Photographic method whereby, optically, a scene fades away and another takes its place.

Go to Black

Empty, black screen.

Freeze

Hold on single frame.

Angle Shot

Any shot other than straight-on.

Split Screen

Two pictures from different cameras on screen at same time.

Wipe

Transition from one scene or image to another in which new scene slowly replaces old one in some gradually increasing geometric

	pattern—for example, circle (iris-in, iris-out), square (expanding square), fan, roll and so on.
2-Shot, 3-Shot and so on	Include two people, three people and so on
Group Shot	Include all people or products.
Over the Shoulder	Shot over shoulder of person to the face of another.
SFX	Sound effects.
Bridge	Links two scenes with music or some effect.
SUPER—Superimpose	Words or numbers that appear over scene.
VO	Narration over action; speaker not in scene.

Hold your audience

Here's one of the big points about writing your TV commercial: you already have your viewer's attention! In the early years of TV, writers from radio and the print world failed to realize this and came on too strong to try to "get" what they usually already had. Like reading a newspaper or magazine, your audience normally sits down and deliberately watches television. Usually it is not a passive medium, as radio is—far from it! Your biggest job at the start of your commercial is to keep the attention you already have instead of driving a viewer off to the kitchen for a snack. Think about that when writing your TV spot.

Script format

You'll find a sample television script and storyboard facing each other on page 144 and 145. Note the style in which the script is typed. At the top is a designation of the client, usually a job number (for billing purposes), the date and a "title"—all scripts get names for handy reference. The first column is labeled

VIDEO and contains a detailed description of the action, including camera directions. This is normally typed all in caps and single spaced. The right-hand column is for the AUDIO portion of the script: the words spoken by the announcer and actors, the music and any sound effects. The audio segments are positioned alongside the video action that corresponds to them.

The storyboard in this example contains the same information as the script. The frames are drawn to match the instructions in the script. Boxes under the frames contain the words to be spoken at that point, along with other audio instructions. A storyboard gives a good indication of the flow of the action and how it's integrated with the statements of product benefits. This is what will be said and done in the final commercial and is the stage when a client first sees the new television commercial.

Getting started

Since television is a merger of words and pictures, a creative concept can originate in either area. However, since all creative activity begins with a verbal statement of objectives (USP), normally the first expression of the creative idea is likewise verbal. It may be a key word, a memorable product description, a slogan—almost anything. It can even be an expression that crosses the boundary between words and pictures—for instance, "What's wrong with strong?" could be a highly visual theme for a mouthwash that's very effective but has a bad-taste drawback. Even as you write in words, you're thinking in pictures.

What form will your commercial take? You have quite a choice: slice-of-life ("slice," for short), presenter, surprise ending, flashback, suspense, interview, competitive comparison, before and after, testimonial, dialogues, cartoon fantasy and probably plenty more that haven't been designed yet! But at this point, you don't know which direction you'll take.

When you've got the key words or statements straightened out in your mind, don't go any further. It would be a mistake to block out a complete script and then go back and try to force the visual action into this mold. Rather, on a blank sheet of scratch paper, quickly rough out some lines in the shape of boxes. Then begin to think visually, drawing stick figures if you lack art talent.

Television is a heavy visual medium. (In fact, if you turn off the sound in a TV commercial, you should understand it just by watching the visual.) Looking at the little blocks on the paper forces you to think in terms of possible scenes. Scribble them in with your own crude art; nobody will see this piece of paper except you. Now, put the paper away at least overnight. Surely you'll have some changes the next morning. Then take a new sheet and tighten up your scenes to a meaningful and workable situation. It's much less expensive now than any time later.

Next, it's back to the typewriter. Who's going to say what? Start to fill in your script sheet. Remember, you've already settled the scene sequence in a general way, at least with yourself. Then take another look at your rough-drawn boxes and determine exactly what type of camera shot you would like for each scene: long shot (LS), close-up (CU) or medium close-up (MCU)? You probably considered this when drawing your rough storyboard. Type the video side of the script sheet. Then get some art help to clean up the storyboard on a standard form, and you should be moving closer to presenting your idea for approval.

Film or tape

It should make no difference to you whether your commercial will be produced on film or on videotape. From a writer's point of view, it's just a matter of different hardware. Your creative thinking will be the same, your script and storyboard will be the same—often the decision which way to go won't be made before this point. The terms we have used so far are the same for both—even the term "frame," which is technically inaccurate for tape because tape contains no frames. So as a copywriter you have no need to be concerned whether your script will be shot on film or tape. However, your work will be made easier if you become familiar with the various technical aspects of filming and taping, including the editing process, which is where significant differences between tape and film occur.

Your first visit to a television studio should be an eye-opener. You'll see how they achieve all those effects in a commercial by merely pushing buttons on the special effects board. Watch what happens when you have two cameras working for you—how you

GOODYEAR TIRE & RUBBER CO.
"BLIMP BEHIND YOU"
:30 TELEVISION
"CHILDREN" (SERVICE CENTERS)

VIDEO	AUDIO
LONG SHOT OF CAR ON HIGHWAY. BLIMP VISIBLE HIGH ABOVE CAR.	MOM: Car's running great, honey.
CUT TO CAR INTERIOR SHOWING FAMILY. BLIMP IS VISIBLE THROUGH REAR WINDOW.	KIDS: We've got the blimp behind us!
CUT TO TIGHT SHOT OF PARENTS TALKING	DAD: Good way to put it. . . haven't had a lick of trouble since I got that tune-up at Goodyear.
CUT TO EXTERIOR SHOT OF CAR, PARTIALLY IN SHADOW.	KIDS: No, it's for real!
CAR TURNS INTO GOODYEAR SERVICE CENTER. SHADOW STILL COVERS PART OF CAR.	DAD: It's real enough for me . . . there are over 1,300 Goodyear Service Centers . . .
CUT TO MECHANIC WORKING ON CAR.	coast to coast.
CUT TO LONG SHOT OF CAR BACK ON HIGHWAY. BLIMP REMAINS OVERHEAD, CASTING SHADOW BEHIND CAR.	MOM: So the blimp's behind us wherever we go.
REPRISE VIDEO #2	KIDS: That's what we've been telling you!
OVERHEAD SHOT OF BLIMP, WITH CAR VISIBLE ON ROAD BELOW. BLIMP'S SHADOW FULLY COVERS CAR.	ANNCR. (VO): The kind of car care you'd expect from the world's leading tire company.
CUT TO FULL SIDE VIEW OF BLIMP. SUPER: "OUT FRONT. WORLD WIDE."	Goodyear. Out front. World wide. MOM: (sounding very uncertain) Honey, what's making that big shadow?

TELEVISION SCRIPT: The writer prepares a commercial in this form before a storyboard is drawn. The "Video" column should describe each scene in as much detail as possible. *Courtesy Goodyear Tire & Rubber Co.*

TELEVISION STORYBOARD: This type of pictorial layout is prepared so that everyone who must approve and complete the commercial can see how the words and action fit together, step by step. *Courtesy Goodyear Tire & Rubber Co.*

can superimpose one scene over the other. Scenes can be video-taped and erased as often as you like until you get the commercial the way you want it.

Your commercial doesn't have to be done live in the TV studio. Sometimes all it requires is marrying some available footage with music and words, together with a good hand at the special effects board. And it could possibly save you all kinds of money and time. The growing use of more mobile equipment—for tape as well as film—makes on-location shooting much easier than it was previously.

All in all, writing for television and radio requires skills that every copywriter should acquire as soon as possible. Invariably, you will be called on to write commercials, and the writer who has become limited to print alone will not have the tools needed to do the job properly. Don't stunt your growth. Plunge into broadcast writing at every opportunity. The more you broaden your experience, the more valuable you become to your present employer—or to your next one!

Campaign planning

9

Why worry about a campaign? Why not let each ad stand on its own two feet, doing the best possible job all by itself? The answer is money. No advertiser—not even the giant soap companies and the auto manufacturers, which are two of the biggest ad spenders in the business—can afford to have each of their ads take off in a different creative direction, even if they all follow the same USP. The waste would be monumental. The only reasonable solution is the development of a campaign to unify the advertising as it's perceived by the consumers.

Campaigns are fundamental to effective advertising. The good ones last for years. "Does she or doesn't she?" started a hair coloring revolution in the 1950s, with Clairol happily leading the way. The "Pepsi Generation" preempted the youth vote for Pepsi. "Marlboro Country," now a part of the language, conjures up romance and imagery that might be diminished by words and has made the cigarette one of the leaders.

A campaign is nothing more than an effort by advertisers to multiply the impact of their advertising dollars. If every ad or commercial were a separate, unique, different platform, can you imagine the confused consumer trying to sort it all out? The fact is, the ads wouldn't be sorted out, they'd be tuned out. For any message to break through the apathy barrier (nobody's out there waiting to read your ad, aside, possibly, from your spouse or friends), it has to become recognized. What a campaign does is contribute a degree of consistency that people eventually become familiar with. Until this click of recognition happens, your advertising is probably not earning its keep; after this point of familiarity is reached, it's a bargain.

Does it strike you as odd that the language of war—"campaign," for instance—has been adopted so avidly by the advertising industry? The marketplace is indeed an epic battlefield where products fight openly for attention and struggle for sales. To survive, you have to have more firepower than the competitors, which comes from a superior product, more aggressive marketing or a combination of both. This applies whether you're a local furniture store competing against a large department store or a major airline locked in competition with other airlines flying the same routes.

COMPETITIVE PRESSURE

Competition is all around you. Competition is probably the cause of those love/hate symptoms you feel: as a businessman, you'd like an open field with no need to keep an eye on the other fellow. But as a consumer, you happily reap the benefits of competition in terms of prices, supply and service. Like it or not, competition is the engine of our economic system, even if it doesn't always work perfectly at all times in all places. And one of the chief weapons a company brings to bear to gain an upper hand is advertising. Not sporadic sorties (occasional ads) that may win a battle now and then, but a sustained offensive (a total ad campaign) that will win the war.

A campaign attempts to bring coherence to the advertising, to give all the ads a common "look." (Or "sound," in the case or radio and television: a musical jingle is one obvious example of a unifying element that's typical of a radio or TV campaign.) This "look" can result from the same typeface for headlines and text. Or from the same artist using the same art style in all the ads. Or from the same overall graphic design of the ads. Generally, but not necessarily, there's something of all three in any given campaign. The test is this: when the ads are all observed side by side, do they all look like they belong in the same family? You're not looking for identical twins, mind you, just for enough basic resemblance—like red hair—to indicate that they all have the same parents.

Along with a consumer campaign, there's often a need for a dealer campaign. This is discussed in the next chapter, "Merchandising Your Advertising."

DON'T EXPECT MIRACLES

It's worth noting again at this time that advertising alone— even if it's a well-conceived, well-financed campaign—is no assurance of success in the marketplace. As mentioned in Chapter 2, advertising is just one part of the marketing mix. At best, it can bring a customer to nibble. After that, the product or service better live up to expectations (what the ad promises) or there will never be a second sale. It's that simple. The landscape is littered with products that failed despite sound advertising and substantial spending. Or as an advertising sage once said, "Good advertising only makes a bad product fail more quickly."

Nevertheless, the force generated by the right advertising at the right time for the right product is awesome. Consider the franchise business, particularly the fast-food operations. The whole concept is based on two pillars: a unique product or style of service plus an exciting, sustained advertising blitz. Everything is coordinated, from national television to the salt and pepper shakers on the tables.

Your well-organized, well-controlled, expertly disciplined advertising campaign should help pull all your advertising efforts together. Ah! But so much easier said than done because you're not usually operating in a vacuum. Normally you'll already have all kinds of assorted advertising messages in the communication channels of newspapers, magazines, radio, TV, point-of-purchase displays, signs, advertising specialities, directories, packaging and so on.

At times it's very difficult for you to get all the continuity and consistency you want because you may already have an old campaign still in the field. Some companies spin off campaigns so rapidly there's always part of one out there; something like the residue from old space shots out in space. This is particularly burdensome when an old slogan is on the product's package. Imagine, for example, the job of just trying to change all the Coca-Cola signs inside stores, outside stores and on trucks, displays, packaging and all the other advertising materials when the company decided to update its logo by adding a new wavy-line design a few years ago.

NATIONAL CAMPAIGNS

What makes plain, everyday, garden-variety advertising different from an advertising campaign? Two things: the fundamental strategy and the actual execution.

On a strategic level, a campaign is an integral part of a company's long-range marketing plans. It comes to grips with the large question: what favorable impression about this product do I want to leave with people who will be exposed to my advertising on a continuous basis over a period of time? (See the discussion of the Unique Selling Proposition in Chapter 4.) For example, a brand of jams and jellies might want to become known as the one that contains no artificial ingredients. From the moment that was decided, all the advertising would hinge on that fact.

Up to now, we have considered only those campaigns for individual products, mostly in the category of "package goods" (what you see lined up like soldiers on the shelves of your local supermarket). Each of these branded items has an identity of its own and its own particular attributes that must be translated into a Unique Selling Proposition. The company that manufactures them is, in most cases, quite irrelevant to the purchaser.

When you pick up a tube of Crest toothpaste, you might think of stannous fluoride or "Look, Ma, no cavities," but thoughts of Procter & Gamble probably never cross your mind. You buy Wheaties because it's the "Breakfast of Champions," not because it's made by General Mills. And if you put a can of Maxwell House coffee in your shopping basket, it's because it's "good to the last drop," while General Foods is simply a tiny name on the label that you can hardly read without a magnifying glass—and who cares anyhow?

COMPANY PROMOTIONS

Aside from campaigns for individual brands, when the parent company is less important, you are probably also familiar with campaigns in which the parent company is all-important. Generally, these overall company campaigns will fall into two categories: advertising a line of products to a clearly defined demographic group, or advertising services when the reputation of the company has a direct link to the preference for the service offered.

Advertising a line of products to a specific demographic group calls for a uniform campaign because these audiences are not normally interested in a single product but rather in a series of different products in the line, probably purchased over a period of time. You want them to associate one product with another and then be favorably inclined to return for another product from the same manufacturer. Consistent advertising plays an important role in this process.

Demographic groups

The following are a few examples to help you get things straight in your own mind.

Farmers are demographically distinct by occupation. Consequently, the advertising directed to them by an implement manufacturer, for instance, would all have a family resemblance. An ad for a hay baler would be designed to be associated with an ad for a forage harvester from the same manufacturer and so on. The advertising thus conceived has a cumulative effect on the target. The similarity of the ads serves to remind the target of the range of different machines the company offers and will often trigger a delayed-action buying decision. Giving ads a common recognition has been shown to increase the awareness of your advertising in excess of the actual dollars spent, which is a very persuasive argument in favor of an ad campaign right there!

There are literally thousands of demographic groups (with

much overlapping) that advertisers aim for, such as "travelers," "do-it-yourselfers," "women who shop at home." Now think about these three target groups. Doesn't the advertising for Samsonite luggage, Black & Decker tools and Avon beauty products indeed follow a campaign format? The rule is this:

> when you've got a variety of related but nevertheless different products (a ¼" drill and a saber saw), and

> when each of these separate products can't of itself justify an advertising expenditure on a level sufficient to make a useful impact, and

> when these products will benefit from association with one another and from a common manufacturer, and

> when these products are of interest to a primary demographic group that can be reached efficiently by selective media,

then the strategy is to marshal your resources and develop a campaign that will give you far more presence among your prospects than you could ever expect from a mixed bag of individual ads for each separate item.

Service campaigns

A campaign approach is also considered essential for somewhat different reasons when you advertise the *services* a company offers. Here you want to convey a feeling of security, of confidence, of trust. Even though there may be various aspects of the service that will get particular attention, the overriding objective is to reassure the reader that she or he is surely making a wise decision to choose what you're offering. When you don't have something tangible to sell, you must continuously remind your audience that it can relax in the certainty that it's doing the right thing.

"You're in good hands with Allstate." Doesn't it comfort you to know someone else is worrying about your insurance so you don't have to?

"Fly the friendly skies of United." A double-barreled effort designed to instill a touch of confidence in those people too timid to fly, while giving the regular business and vacation traveler a good reason—friendly, courteous service—to prefer United over the competition.

"Reach out and touch someone." AT&T was highly successful in proving that long-distance calling was not an extravagance, but rather a close-at-hand means of bringing people closer together. It makes you want to call someone far away and feel good when you do. This whole idea was captured in five memorable words.

INSTITUTIONAL ADVERTISING

When a corporation feels a need to make *itself* the "product," the result is institutional advertising. It's also called corporate advertising or public relations advertising, and less formally it's known as image advertising. The purpose of a program such as this is to present the organization in a favorable light by drawing attention to some of its positive attributes or contributions that would not normally get the requisite attention. Corporate advertising is usually planned as part of a total public relations effort (see Chapter 2). What makes it unique and essential in the eyes of management is the fact that only by advertising can the company be sure that its message will appear where and when it's wanted and in exactly the form the company chooses. Corporate advertising lets a company put its best foot forward with little chance of misstep.

There are several reasons why a company would want to advertise itself like this. General goodwill is one: an organization hopes to gain an edge in "popularity" that ultimately could be translated into sales. Or a company may find it necessary to counteract bad publicity (potentially damaging to sales) by advertising its positive features that get overlooked in the news columns. Still other corporate campaigns are designed to make "influence leaders" (legislators) see the company's point of view or are aimed at the business community in an effort to make the company's stock more attractive. While one or more such primary objectives is always present, institutional advertising invariably boosts employee morale, too. The smart corporate advertiser makes sure the ads are posted prominently where employees can see them.

Whatever Happened To "Yes, Please"?

It went
the way of
"Thank you,"
"Excuse me,"
"Yes, sir."
Do you know
who just about
killed all those
phrases?
All of us.
We did not use
them enough.
We now get
"Huh?"
"What?"
"Gimme more."
Mannerly responses
are learned at home.
Rude, barbaric
responses also are
learned at home.
William of Wykeham,
who was born in 1324,
said, "Manners
maketh man."
If we're
so smart
in the
20th century,
how come
we're not
as civilized
as William was
in the
14th century?
To the child
who says,
"Huh?"
pass along this page.

BY PRESENTING ITS VIEWPOINT on a small social question, this corporation seeks to show that its concerns go beyond those traditionally associated with large, impersonal organizations. *Courtesy United Technologies Corporation.*

"As a chemist who helps decide how industry wastes are managed, my standards are high. As a father, even higher."

TO BRING ITS SIDE of an issue before the public, a company or other organization often turns to advertising. *Courtesy Chemical Manufacturers Association.*

Just seeing "my company" advertising itself is a big source of pride to workers.

Institutional advertising is not confined to corporations. Industry associations (Institute of Life Insurance), unions (Teamsters) and special interest groups (National Rifle Association) are among those who use the clout of a well-conceived, well-programmed corporate campaign. Corporate advertising for public service purposes is very common, too. The Advertising Council was formed to provide a structure that would support a continuing series of national public service campaigns for nonprofit groups—the American Red Cross, Smokey the Bear and United States Savings Bonds are all Ad Council "clients" (for which the creative work is done free by various advertising agencies and the time or space is donated by the media). Local communities likewise sponsor a variety of public service programs, and you can expect excellent cooperation from the local media (especially radio and TV stations, who must, by law, provide a certain amount of public service time for nonprofit organizations). Supporting such commendable campaigns is also good "public relations" for a station owner or a publisher.

Don't expect instant results from institutional advertising. Its results may not be noticed for years. It's not slam-bang; it has to sink in slowly. Consistency is the key word; the strongest USP must be developed right at the start. As a copywriter, you'll be working with the campaign for years, so it's crucial that the USP be correct or else your efforts may go down the drain.

RETAIL CAMPAIGNS

All that has been said so far relating to ad campaigns for national advertisers applies equally to local retail establishments. This is an area where consistency is often neglected because the major emphasis is usually on price.

There's no question that local retail advertising will always have more urgency to it—for example, "Last Week of White Sale!" Normally retail themes (usually stated as slogans) are much more short-lived in comparison to national corporate efforts. The store could have a campaign that lasts for a week, for a month or for a specific season such as the Christmas season or back-to-school time. Retail campaigns can also become necessary when the store makes a special purchase, putting pressure on sales to reduce inventory . . . or by management's decision to start a trend—whether it be a new fashion style or imports from China. Such programs are relatively short-term in execution but still call for a concerted storewide effort: a campaign. Even so, never forget the cardinal rule of retail advertising—shoppers want bargains. And they always will.

The major advertising principles, however, remain the same. After all, both the national and the local advertiser want the same thing—more business at the lowest possible cost. It's simply that everything is more urgent at the local level, that's all. Since the main objectives of national and local advertisers are the same and since the audience for the advertising is the same, why should the advertising principles be any different?

Retail tactics

While general campaign principles remain the same, some details will be different. For one thing, the overall goal of a local retail campaign is to increase store traffic and to generate excitement for the store rather than for individual items. Impulse buying is very important to retailers. (Branded products and their national advertising play a big role here, by the way.) The retailer's goal is to build traffic and then make the buying attractive. Retail advertising usually places more emphasis on seasonal and special events, too. Remember that any way you can exploit national advertising for key items gives added impetus to your efforts. Why reinvent the wheel every day?

The following are some things that can be coordinated for a more successful retail campaign. Not all of them may be the responsibility of the retail copywriter, but you should be aware of all the possibilities.

- all the media advertising—introduction of special media for special events (outdoor? radio?)

- window displays

- interior displays

- special direct mail

- charge account stuffers

- postage-machine imprints

- elevator signs

- tent signs for dining room tables

- headers for racks

- public address announcements

- buttons for store personnel to wear

- special wrapping paper and packaging.

If you're a copywriter who likes a lot of action, then you'll thrive on your involvement in a full-scale retail campaign like this.

Building image

More attention could possibly be devoted to changing people's *attitudes* about your local client with an eye toward forming a firm *image* of the business in people's minds. What kind of merchandise or service do they offer? What do people think about the business today? Are they correct? Or have they misunderstood? Would you like them to perceive the business differently in the future?

For instance, a clothing chain decided to use its lack of fancy decor to reinforce its low-price policy. Its "plain pipe racks" advertising theme soon became synonymous with bargains. Another store, one whose forte was its extraordinary selection of merchandise that others couldn't match, exploited this advantage neatly: "Select, don't settle" became its very successful slogan. On the other hand, a major New York department store in the popular price range long ago saw the opportunity to upgrade its image and flatter its customers at the same time. "It's smart to be thrifty," proclaimed all of its advertising, and it's probably an idea that will never go out of style.

None of these businesses had to forego price promotions while they were in the process of establishing their image with their audiences. Even a high-fashion establishment, where price is seemingly secondary, can have similar types of campaigns. All the advertising that a store like this prepares should be a conscious effort to support the high-price image. For instance, certain art treatments suggest "elegance" better than others. The same goes for typefaces. Even the generous use of white space in the design of the layouts can contribute to the luxurious, fashionable—and expensive—image the store wants to convey to an audience that seeks this kind of atmosphere.

Long-range goals

The whole idea is for a store to keep its eye on its long-range goals even while courting today's customers. This takes a certain amount of discipline. Everybody would like to be all things to all people, to presume that the whole universe represents the potential pool of customers available. Deep-down you probably know this is wishful thinking, but the urge to believe otherwise is often overwhelming.

If there's something unique about your business, say so. Again and again. If your merchandise or service is different in any way, make this clear—consistently. If you feature high-fashion or budget prices, if your prime advantage is convenient location or expanded hours, if you see any way that your business fills a need unmet—or unpublicized—by your competition, make sure your advertising program stresses this distinction.

Room still remains for news of sales, special events and other traffic-building devices that are the lifeblood of the retail trade. But even while this is going on, why not look further down the road? Decide how you want people to picture you. Be sure your business can live up to this image. Then make sure that your advertising says this with conviction and conveys this same idea by its overall appearance. The ideal campaign for a local advertiser contains a memorable, meaningful verbal theme that unmistakably identifies the image you want to portray, coupled with a visual treatment that reinforces this theme. All this will be linked, of course, to the inevitable "sale" or some other special promotion.

THE IMPORTANCE OF BEING DIFFERENT

What do you do if your client's business is essentially identical with his competition? Here you must create a difference that somehow makes it more desirable to patronize your client instead of the others. A New York bank proclaimed for years, "You have a friend at Chase Manhattan." True enough. But you probably had a similar friend at every other bank in town, too. But Chase preempted friendship to its distinct advantage for many years. A Florida home care center, with the same basic do-it-yourself merchandise as other such establishments, says, "You can do it with Lindsley's help." It's a simple note of encouragement and support that probably could have been promised equally by the competition—but wasn't. So Lindsley is now known as "the store that helps you," which is certainly a valuable reputation that translates into sales. In each case, the advertiser established an image, stated it in a way that filled a perceived need in the minds of its potential customers—and then stuck to its guns for years.

Consistency, continuity and repetition—that's the bedrock on which advertising campaigns are built! So take your time before proceeding. Give serious thought to what you are and where you're going. Allow ample time for the planning and the execution of the advertising that will carry this idea. If you end up on the right track—allowing sufficient time for the idea to take hold— you should have a campaign that will successfully represent you for a long time.

SLOGANS

Slogans, or stated themes, are often used to hold a campaign together. When appropriate, slogans can often run through more than one campaign. If they do, they're used more as identification than as an integral part of the new campaign. A good slogan should be framed in such a way that it's unique in its own way and is not easily adaptable to a competitor's product. Ideally, the name of the advertiser should be built into the slogan. There should be no opportunity to forget who's inviting you to try the service. Sounds basic enough, doesn't it? But just thumb through a copy of the nearest magazine and you'll see how frequently this factor is ignored. Sometimes the sheer weight of advertising dollars can overcome this failing. But conversely, you can often win the same recognition with fewer dollars if you include the name of the sponsor in the campaign theme.

Slogans are usually short and easy to remember. For example, "Delta is ready when you are," "Tide's in, dirt's out" or "Take Aim against cavities." Use any grammatical device in the book to help make the slogan stick: alliteration, rhyme, a special cadence—anything. You must force people to remember the slogan against their will, so use every way possible. Slogans are "buywords." They're worth all the time and trouble it takes to invent them.

UNSTATED THEMES

The Unique Selling Proposition, of course, is the bedrock on which everything else is built. A slogan is a development of the USP. But a slogan isn't always necessary—it isn't the only string that ties a campaign together. Sometimes your copy approach can accomplish this by itself. So can the graphics you select, the placement of elements in the ad design, the colors used, the logo treatment or the plot structure for radio and television commercials. The famous campaign that made Volkswagen a household word had no stated theme, no slogan. So it is with many other major manufacturers—Kodak and RCA, to name two—who have traditionally relied on creating a product personality rather than counting on slogans to hold their campaigns together.

Volkswagen made up for the absence of a slogan in several extraordinary ways. Studies show that the ads are recognizable from 20 to 30 feet away—a graphic coup that would make any competitor envious. The copy was skillfully crafted—simple sentences, no wasted words, utter frankness, no overstatements (except for humorous effect) and specific, believable claims.

Volkswagen also taught the industry a thing or two about consistency. In the very beginning VW settled on a strong USP ("the car that offers the best value for the money") and stuck with it for years. And only one specific idea was used per ad: resale value, traction, easy parking, good gas mileage, less maintenance and so on. But none of the advertising ever lost sight of the USP. Each ad in each medium emphasized the fact that Volkswagen was the best value for the money. Value may have been costumed as "economy," or "reliability" or even "status," but a reader always came away with the feeling that Volkswagen was a smart idea. There's a lot to be learned from this famous case history.

STATE YOUR OBJECTIVES

Never try to write a word of copy without first reaching agreement on what the campaign is attempting to communicate. This agreement must be very clear and very specific. Get it in writing! (What short memories people have when it suits their purposes!) Depending on the advertiser, this agreement is called different names. A Copy Platform is a rather elaborate agreement in most cases. It outlines the goals of the campaign, the chief benefits, facts and figures that support these benefits, a description of the market for the product and sometimes an indication of the media schedule that can help accomplish all this. A basic Copy Platform might include the following:

Objectives. The *strategy*—what you're trying to accomplish

Proposition. The *benefit*—the basis of your appeal

Rationale. The *features*—supporting evidence for benefit

Target Audience. The *market*—the likeliest prospects for your product

This basic Copy Platform should be adequate in most situations. In any event, the platform is a rather long document that requires the approval and agreement of a wide range of people, which takes time. For this reason, one of the following brief agreements is frequently all that is required to launch the creative work.

A Copy Proposition is a shorter statement that simply spells out, in straightforward language, what makes the product different and therefore more desirable to a potential purchaser. The following might serve as a sample format for a Copy Proposition:

> (name of dog food) is (the easiest to serve) because (it's packaged in individual servings) .

There's no excess baggage here. The more single-minded you are, the better your chances of developing strong advertising.

A Copy (or Creative) Strategy is a concise statement of the objectives of the campaign and what there is about the product that makes these objectives attainable. A typical Copy Strategy often takes this form:

> To convince (mothers of small children) that (name of product) will (make their children brush their teeth more often) because (it tastes so good they'll be happy to use it) .

A Position is a brief description of how the product answers a need previously unidentified and therefore unfilled. A position statement, in effect, seeks to create a market group and then finds the product characteristics that can best appeal to this market. A Position results from the following analysis: For a new product (for example, a shampoo with extra hair conditioners), you might isolate a market segment (women who are harming their hair by excessive blow-drying and hot curlers) by making an appeal such as "Here's a shampoo that will restore health to heat-damaged hair." In other words, you've "positioned" the product as the one that's especially formulated to answer a need that was never before specifically identified.

No matter what it's called, this type of creative planning is an essential first step. Make sure everyone concerned is in clear agreement on objectives. Then and only then can you proceed to the Unique Selling Proposition, framing this appeal in terms that give the product the best chance to accomplish the stated objective. Your USP will be nothing more than an extraction of the single strongest selling point, based on the product's composition, the competitive environment and the nature of the audience you're appealing to.

Naturally, since a USP is so fundamental to everything else, many people get into the act before one is drafted. On the manufacturer's side, you can expect to find the product manager, the advertising manager, a representative from market research and often someone involved with the sales force—in short, just about everyone who knows about the product and the market. On the agency side, you have the account executive, the creative director and sometimes a specialist in merchandising. The makeup of the group will vary according to the product.

The easy part is collecting the input. The hard part is agreeing on the single most promotable feature, which means making everything else secondary. The word "promotable" is vital. You may have, for example, a shampoo that gets hair measurably cleaner, but before you start celebrating, you learn that studies show women (or men) are invariably very satisfied with the way their present shampoo cleans their hair. There's no use following a good road that goes nowhere so it's back to the drawing board. The search goes on for something else your product is able to offer, something that is more likely to make the market react. (Chapter 4 describes how to develop a USP.)

Avoid piecemeal campaigns or fragmented campaign planning. Visualize all the elements for the campaign before starting one of them. Most corporations or agencies schedule all the jobs at once to avoid any possible slippage. After continuity and consistency, the last element a campaign requires is repetition. This, of course, depends heavily on the advertising budget and the skill of the media buyer.

CAMPAIGN LIFE

How long should a campaign run? A good question. It's a difficult decision but one that often is based on the available budget, competitive activity, seasonal considerations and sales indicators. It's wasteful to change a campaign just for the sake of change, which happens too often. Interestingly, you can usually tell when advertisers have a good campaign going: they leave it alone. One advertisement by a famous Pennsylvania inn used the headline "If you can't be a house guest in Bucks County, be ours," over and over, unchanged, for years (see p. 32). The Clairol "Does She or Doesn't She?" campaign has run in one form or another

Aren't you glad you use Dial?

Dial,® the best-selling deodorant soap, has twice the active deodorant ingredient as the #2 brand.

<u>Twice</u> as much to get rid of the bacteria that cause odor.

And <u>twice</u> as much to keep you feeling clean. Fresh. And confident. All day long.

And all in a formula that's mild and gentle enough for your whole family to use.

Aren't you glad?

Dial. With twice the active deodorant ingredient.

LONG-RUNNING CAMPAIGN: For over a generation, Dial has been identified with this headline. When you've got something good, stick with it. *Courtesy Armour-Dial, Inc.*

for over a quarter century. "Aren't you glad you use Dial?" is another classic that has been around almost as long.

When your product has been fortunate to find an advertising campaign that works, count your blessings and save all those other great ideas for another day. When you find something that works, stick with it.

Your own management can be responsible for killing a campaign too soon. While this is easy to understand, it's unfortunate because it confuses dealers and consumers and eats up advertising dollars. "Give us something new!" is usually the cry. Or, "What, that same old commercial on TV!"

Sales reps, too, succumb to the feeling that a campaign is "old" long before it has been given its planned exposure. That's one reason it's wise to build sales contests and dealer contests into your campaign planning. This will be a big help in keeping enthusiasm high despite intensive exposure to the "same" campaign. As you'll discover, a campaign wears out much more slowly with the public than it does with the executives, sales force and dealers who live with it day in and day out.

There often can be a sleeper (delayed) effect in determining the success of your advertising campaign. Sometimes the consumer isn't ready to purchase floor polish or a new refrigerator when he or she notices your ad or sees your commercial. Your advertising message may not pay out until months after your last ad appears.

Retailers know that weather can raise havoc with their sales, despite the advertising. A bad snowstorm or three days of rain can cut deeply into what would have been better results. In addition, be sure to review all the other ingredients in a marketing mix, other than advertising, that can reduce the effect of your advertising campaign.

Flights

Some companies that produce many different products schedule their advertising campaigns in "flights." This means that each product in turn gets a major share of the total available advertising budget for a specified period of time. The advantage is that during this concentrated time period, the product gets maximum exposure to the target audience. The company's other products, meanwhile, are waiting their turn for the same revolving support. This flight concept gives selected products increased exposure for a specified time. Otherwise, the advertising budget would be stretched so thin among so many different products that it would be hard for any one of them to achieve any sizable impact. Normally there's also a sustaining budget for each product when it does not have access to the flight funds. This is a particularly interesting way to fund campaigns for highly competitive packaged goods.

Local follow-up

Occasionally retailers become the missing link in national advertising campaigns. This is not entirely the retailer's fault. Some manufacturers still do not realize the importance of a strong effort at the local level and so do not offer appropriate tie-in advertising and promotional material that the retailer can use. If you're a copywriter in a retail situation, you'll miss this support when it's lacking. If you're writing for a manufacturer or for an agency, you should not let this opportunity pass by.

Tie-in advertising is discussed in greater detail in Chapter 10, "Merchandising Your Advertising." But for now, it's urged that manufacturers make available to retail outlets that carry their products such materials as admats (ads that are shipped to dealers for reproduction in local newspapers), display materials, envelope stuffers, radio scripts—and maybe even TV spots with space for a dealer tag. This all means using similar graphics with copy written from a retail viewpoint. Needless to say, a main thrust of the national campaign should be to get continuity, consistency and repetition at the local level.

NON-CAMPAIGN ADS

Exceptions make the (advertising) world go round. For example, if you're in a retail copywriting situation, the day-to-day pace is so swift that you're frequently forced to do a one-shot ad. Fair enough. Still, you should make every effort to connect it to what has gone before—with the Logo, slogan (if one exists), type selection and anything else that a reader might be able to relate to your previous advertising. Give your ad every edge possible!

Or as a member of a corporate advertising department, you'll undoubtedly have many things to do that are unrelated to any advertising campaign that's underway. (Your advertising agency will be largely responsible for that.) You'll find yourself involved in writing product literature and keeping it up to date, writing admats, writing radio spots and designing (along with an art director) posters and other sales promotional material. While all this material presents the company to the public, there's a good chance each project will be done at a different time to meet different deadlines. What often happens in this case is that they become separate entities lacking a common bond. You should strive to tie all these efforts as closely as possible to the national advertising, to the campaign as presented to the public. Exceptions should be just that—exceptions.

Agency copywriters will also occasionally be asked to do a job that departs from the campaign trail. An individual ad that's not part of the campaign usually has a more immediate and utilitarian objective. Advertisers may supplement their campaigns in this way in response to a specific marketing problem, whether it's a surplus inventory situation or competitive pressure of some sort or other. A campaign is supposed to boost the effectiveness of advertising, not block it. So it must always be flexible enough to be adjusted swiftly to situations that weren't anticipated when the original plan was made.

Furthermore, just because an ad is a part of an ongoing campaign, there's nothing to prevent it from being powerful and persuasive all by itself. It's true, however, that any advertising that follows a prescribed format does have certain restrictions, and the man or woman who is creating the advertising sacrifices some creative freedom. But you've got to remember that the objective of any advertising is to make someone see things your way. Nothing else matters. Advertising is not an art form. It's communication. It's persuasion. Everything else takes a back seat.

Merchandising your advertising
10

"Merchandising" your advertising merely means making every effort to get extra mileage out of it—that is, getting your advertising seen, talked about, noticed or displayed before, during or after its appearance in a magazine or newspaper. This merchandising concept can, and should, also be applied to your commercials on radio and television.

Merchandising takes two main forms. First, there are programs designed to drum up enthusiasm in your sales force and distributor/dealer organizations. The backing of both these groups is essential if they're going to push a little bit harder in your behalf. And they will, too, if you show them all the advertising support they're going to get from the "factory." Remember, rarely are retailers selling only your product—they're probably selling your competitor's, too!

Second, efforts are made to remind potential customers of your advertising that they've already seen or heard. The pages in a publication get turned pretty fast, your ad along with them. Commercials are over in a minute or less. How can you get a

169

longer run for your message and your company's advertising dollars?

"SELLING" THE SALES FORCE

Before your advertising program is launched, you'll undoubtedly be asked to help merchandise it to your own sales personnel. This will often get you involved in the preparation of presentations for the sales meeting where the new campaign will be unveiled, including slides, charts, banners, balloons and all the other hoopla that has come to be expected at these sessions.

As a part of this, you'll probably be required to help prepare a sales presentation that will explain the new consumer advertising program together with a flock of ideas that the individual dealer can use to make the most of all this ad support. A typical presentation kit of this kind might include preprints (early printings) of ads that will be run in the campaign, samples of new product literature, radio spots (scripts, discs or tapes), admats, descriptions of TV spots that are available, pictures of banners for store use, samples of bill stuffers for monthly charge account mailings, equipment stickers to emphasize new features, sample "open house" letters that dealers can mail to their customers to introduce new models, illustrations of POP materials and posters, and lists of low-cost advertising specialties.

You may also want to include some market facts (from your research department), such as sales forecasts by month, opportunity areas, replacement buyers versus first-time buyers and a host of other useful data that computers now make accessible. You can include almost anything that will make dealers conclude that the manufacturer is helping them make more profit with your line. It's also not unusual to include the proposed media plan, which indicates the timing and the placement of the advertising as well as the number of viewers, listeners and readers this will deliver.

Just remember that room for making presentations is often limited in most dealers' offices, so plan accordingly. Also, some of your sales reps may dislike the idea of hauling around visual-aid equipment when their dealers are mostly in big cities where parking spaces are an unpleasantly long walk from the dealer's or buyer's office. Some sales reps will tell you they never use the materials. Don't let this bother you too much. Even though the material may sometimes stay in car trunks, you can be sure the sales reps will review it and learn many good talking points from all your efforts.

One word of caution: never make it appear that all your advertising efforts leave nothing for the dealer to do except sit back and collect money. Both of you know better than that!

Preparing materials for presentations can be one of the more satisfying aspects of your job because you're teaming up with the sales and marketing departments to generate excitement for the new advertising that will soon be breaking. Building a high degree of esprit de corps is the goal of every corporation—and here you are, right in the middle of it!

ENLISTING DEALER SUPPORT

You'll also develop a theme to excite dealers, help solicit their interest and encourage them to help make the company's efforts a success. To do all this you must clearly communicate to the dealers what's in it for them, as explained in Chapter 4. Ideally, you'll be able simply to adjust or add to the consumer theme a thought that's meaningful to dealers. For example, if your consumer theme were "Here Comes the Big One," your dealer theme might say "Here Comes the Big One for More Profit." In this way there is a cohesiveness between your advertising for dealers and consumers. This "extends" your advertising in a very effective way. Every time dealers see your consumer ads or watch your commercials, they'll be reminded of what's in it for them. Remember, in most distribution systems, you have to help sell the dealer before you can sell a consumer; you've got to sell *in* (win shelf space or floor space) before a dealer can sell *out* (complete a sale for your product).

It should be mentioned again that dealers are not always *exclusive* dealers; many also sell your competitor's products. It then becomes a challenge to compete directly with your competition for the same dealer's time, interest and space. Often dealers' purchasing patterns are based on which company most heavily supports their selling efforts.

Kenney-supplied stores make more profit.
Again.

A few years ago a major study showed that you make more profit carrying Kenney than any other known brand.

But things change. Shoppers change. Product lines change. So it was time for a new study ... which shows more strongly than ever that your top supplier is Kenney.

Why? Because to our line of over 3,000 drapery hardware products we've been steadily adding new and exciting alternative lines. First, two complete new lines of roll-ups, woven woods and Roman shades. And also window shades.

Each line has new displays, new

packaging—a complete sales and service program. Each is backed by a field service program that gives you restock shipments in 24 hours, and by an advertising program that helps you sell.

Send for your free copy of "The Advent of Alternatives." It is practically a textbook on how to sell today's shopper the new mix of window treatment products—and make a profit doing it.

Write Kenney Mfg. Co., 1000 Jefferson Blvd., Warwick, R.I. 02887, or call toll free (800) 556-6531.

Get the facts

THE PROFIT MOTIVE is what moves dealers to stock your line and promote your products at the point of sale. When you've got a good story, tell the trade about it. *Courtesy Kenney Manufacturing Co.*

Complete merchandising of your advertising also requires you to prepare collateral (tie-in) materials for your dealers to help complete the marketing "sell-through" at the local level right to the consumer. You'll do this by creating admats (slicks or repro-proofs), radio spots and sometimes TV commercials. The consumer campaign theme should be very evident in these materials that are prepared to help merchandise the national advertising campaign at the local level.

More aggressive manufacturers also make complete window displays available to dealers, including all the props needed to tie into the current consumer advertising campaign. Others send sketches with suggestions on how to do it. Still others offer cash incentives if the dealer puts in the suggested window, takes a snapshot of it and mails the picture to the manufacturer or gives it to the sales representative.

Through the use of these collateral materials and other merchandising efforts, you can more successfully link the local dealer directly to your national campaign so that your total ad effort comes to a focus at the point of sale.

CO-OP ADVERTISING

This term is a shortened form of "cooperative advertising," so called because it is an effort in which both the retailer and the manufacturer share the cost. The retailer arranges for the advertising and, provided this advertising meets the conditions specified in the existing "Cooperative Advertising Agreement," is reimbursed according to prescribed terms by the manufacturer.

Many companies make programs of this kind available to their customers. When they do, the Robinson-Patman Act requires that they make the same terms available to all of their customers in a given trade area. This will not directly concern you as a copywriter, but an understanding of this point will be useful to you in your overall approach to this subject.

It may surprise you to know that $5 billion was spent in co-op advertising in 1981, according to industry estimates. Much of the retail advertising you see in newspapers was probably funded (at least in part) by co-op dollars. This even includes the

1981 COOPERATIVE
ADVERTISING PROGRAM

Maximum Dollars Allowed—
Wolverine World Wide will pay up to 50% of net space and time cost of all approved dealer advertising up to 2% of net dollar shipments on regular current merchandise. The terms and conditions of this co-op policy as set forth below may not be modified. No one is authorized to make any exceptions.

Effective Dates—
On all approved advertising from January 1 thru December 31, 1981.

Approved Advertising
Newspapers—
Net paid general circulation daily, Sunday and weekly that meet the following qualifications are authorized under this program.

    a. Specifically serve the retailer's trading area
    b. Meet second-class mailing privileges
    c. Retail rates and circulation are verifiable through independent audit

Radio and Television—
Advertising time costs are allowable only on spot announcements prepared by Wolverine World Wide. All others require prior approval. Any requests must be sent to the Advertising Department, Wolverine World Wide, Rockford, Michigan, and include the following:

    a. Audio script and/or storyboard
    b. Station(s) to be used
    c. Total spots to be aired with specific time schedule to determine costs
    d. Local rate card and total cost of announcements to be run

Final approval of advertising and total costs must be received from the Advertising Department, Wolverine World Wide, Rockford, Michigan, before scheduling.

Other Media—
Any request for use of other media must be sent to the Advertising Department, Wolverine World Wide, Rockford, Michigan and include the following:

    a. Media and layout
    b. Circulation/distribution/location
    c. Full cost/our share

PLEASE NOTE:
No Advertising Claim Deductions can be made from merchandise invoices in accordance with Federal Trade Commission Guidelines on Cooperative Advertising. In order to avoid the possibility that you/or Wolverine will be in violation of the F.T.C. Guidelines, we will suspend shipments to your account in the event of co-op allowance deductions from our invoices.

Qualified Advertising—
1. Wolverine* brand name must be used prominently in the advertisement. If the brand name appears only in the body copy, the ad will not be acceptable.
2. The brand name Wolverine˙ must be used and followed by a generic reference boot and/or shoes.
3. All ads must carry ® indicating that the brand name WOLVERINE* and the WOLVERINE* animal symbol are registered trademarks. Use only this logo as shown.
4. ADS MUST SHOW PRODUCT AND BRAND NAME PROMINENTLY. Combination ads showing or mentioning other merchandise will be pro-rated according to the space devoted to WOLVERINE˙ boots and shoes.
5. Maximum allowed for any ad is 50% of the ad cost.
6. No payment will be made for advertising in any other media, without advance approval of Wolverine World Wide or the Advertising Checking Bureau.
7. To be honored, ALL CLAIMS MUST BE SUBMITTED WITHIN 60 DAYS AFTER ADVERTISING APPEARS.
8. This program applies to WOLVERINE˙ brand boots and shoes only.

Documentation—
Newspapers—Copy of paid invoice with tearsheet bearing name and date of the newspaper.
Radio and Television—Copy of the station invoice detailing length of commercial, its cost, and the total cost at lowest contract rate less discounts. Each script broadcast must be attached and bear station certification as to the times broadcast. Following the ANA/RAB and ANA/TvB approved formats as specified on the back of this form.

Co-op Claim Procedure
Deadlines—
All claims must be submitted within 60 days after advertising appears.

Claims returned for additional information will not be paid unless they are re-submitted within 60 days.

Co-op Claim Procedure—
Submit all Cooperative Advertising Claims with this form No. ACB-2 to:

    Wolverine˙ Boots and Shoes
    The Advertising Checking Bureau
    Box 8434
    Columbus, Ohio 43201

                        Form: ACB-2
                        Revised: 1/81

A TYPICAL CO-OP AGREEMENT spells out the various conditions that must be met by retail advertisers in order for their claims to qualify for the co-op allowance. *Courtesy Wolverine World Wide, Inc.*

"omnibus" ads favored by food stores and drug chains where dozens of different products are displayed.

Since so many dollars are spent in this area, a great deal of advertising must be prepared to meet this need. If you are a writer for a company providing this material, here are some of the things you should bear in mind:

- Be sure the product artwork you provide is of reproduction quality. It should be offered in various sizes because the idea is to encourage retailers to clip it out and you don't know what size they'll need.

- If the product logo is important, once again supply the appropriate artwork in a variety of sizes so the store can clip and use the size it wants. Since retailers often use the product art and skip the logo, you might even consider slightly overlapping the logo on the product art so it can't be neglected in the ad.

- Since you're offering artwork, why not copy as well? Retailers may welcome this assistance—and you'll be sure they use the correct description. But keep it crisp. Get right to the point. No wasted words.

If you're a copywriter for a retail store, you should know what co-op material is available. It may be more than you think. By making use of existing art or photographs, you could save a lot of money. And if you can't find exactly what you need, try phoning the manufacturer to see if it can be provided.

As a retail copywriter, you'll also be in a position to make sure to use correctly any products for which co-op funds are expected. You should be familiar with the terms of the Co-op Agreement. Is the manufacturer's logo required? Must the complete trademark name appear? Must the picture be a certain size? If all the conditions of the Co-op Agreement are not met, it's possible that your advertising won't qualify for the co-op allowance your store is counting on. So be sure to check things out before you start.

How are co-op claims processed? Proof of performance (usually a newspaper tearsheet) is mailed to the manufacturer or to an audit service that handles this service for the manufacturer.

To: The Publisher and Advertising Manager

Dear Friends:

Here's another opportunity for some extra lineage!

May we suggest that you call on your local __(advertiser)__
dealer and urge him to tie-in with the current __(advertiser)__
campaign in the Nebraska Farmer.

This mat and proof are being mailed to you for that purpose and
we suggest you have them with you when you make this call.

You may be sure we are glad to mail this material to you.
It seems like a splendid idea to coordinate advertising and
selling.

Good luck! Please let us know if we can give you additional
information.

Thanks and best wishes, we are

Sincerely yours,

Martha Baldus
Merchandising Manager

Encl.

NEBRASKA   FARMER   COMPANY
A SUBSIDIARY OF HARCOURT BRACE JOVANOVICH, INC.
STREET ADDRESS: 5601 O STREET, LINCOLN, NEBRASKA 68510 ■ MAILING ADDRESS: P.O. BOX 81208, LINCOLN, NEBRASKA 68501
TELEPHONE 402/489-9331

A MAGAZINE CAN MULTIPLY the effect of your advertising by seeking
local dealer newspaper ads that relate to the national advertising. *Courtesy Nebraska Farmer Company.*

There the advertising is checked for compliance and, if satisfactory, evaluated based on the rates the retailer paid for the space. The company receives this information and reimburses the retailer in whole or in part according to the agreement. The same procedure is followed for radio and television co-op claims, except that a copy of the script and the station log showing when the commercials aired constitutes the necessary proof of performance.

MEDIA ASSISTANCE

It's always nice to get help with your job, particularly if the help is free or almost free! Most major media, notably magazines, have ad merchandising plans. These plans include dealer mailings, which range from the magazine sending an actual issue with your ad thumbcut (marked) to your dealers to sending a preprint to all your dealers or sending a blow-up of the ad for use as a poster by the dealer in the store's windows or interior. Your ad can be merchandised to your dealers on counter cards (stand-up signs) that are printed and mailed by the magazine. For most of these services there may be a nominal charge made by the medium but it may be free—if you ask.

Often each of these efforts is accompanied by a letter from the publication on its own stationery. This, in itself, adds to the impact on the dealer, who probably receives mail from your company often but less frequently from publications. Sometimes dealers are more interested in a letter on a popular magazine's stationery than in one on your own company's, even though the letters contain the same information—the novelty factor at work!

The mechanics for merchandising your advertising via the medium are as easy as providing a mailing list of your dealers— and making arrangements far enough in advance!

Still another interesting way to merchandise your advertising is to let the publication mail reprints of your ads to special-interest groups, sometimes in sufficient quantity for distribution to their members if you feel the communication is worth the extra cost. For example, a magazine can easily send your material to home economics teachers (if you want to disseminate your food advertising). Other such special-interest groups and opinion leaders exist for almost any product. And when they get material on an unex-

A CHECKLIST OF CBS MERCHANDISE SERVICES

☐ **Print Communications**

Posters	Program Write-ups
Sales Letters	Calendars/Schedules
Marketing Presentations	Brochures/Folios
Audience Analysis	Point of Purchase Displays

☐ **Audio Visual Communications**

Video Presentations	Promotional Slides/Tapes
Cassette Mini-presentations	Marketing and Audience
Program Clips	Information Slides
Audio Presentations	

☐ **CBS Sports Communications**

PGA Tour, NBA, NFL Gift Items	"The Champions on CBS" Sports
Sports Program Video Material	Poster Series
Talent Appearances	

☐ **Tickets to CBS Sponsorship Events**

Sports Events	Music & Entertainment
Award Programs	Events

☐ **Hospitality Services**

Coordination with CBS Hospitality	Independent Arrangements
Functions	

☐ **PGA Tour on CBS Merchandise Activity**

Golf Tournament Tickets	PGA Tour Gifts
& Hospitality	CBS Souvenir Gifts:
Pro-Am Participations	Golf Balls,
Pro Golf Clinics	Periscopes, Umbrellas
Co-op Posters	Broadcast Facility Tours

☐ **Talent In-Person/Videotape**

CBS Sports and Entertainment
   Talent

☐ **CBS Identification Gifts**

Tennis & Golf Balls	Casio Mini-Calculator & Stopwatch
Cross Date/Time Pens*	Casio Date/Time Lucite Clocks*
Cross Pen	Lucite Desk Sets*
Key Ring*	Umbrellas
Glassware*	Lapel & Stick Pins*
Tote Bags	Magnifying Glass/Paper Weight*
Duffle Bag	* New Items (1981)

☐ **Related Tie-In Promotions**

Records	Advertising Specialty Merchandise
Books	Posters

A SPECTRUM OF MERCHANDISING SERVICES is made available to CBS television sponsors. Such promotional specialties serve to remind the trade of the advertiser's association with CBS and how this will, in turn, support retail sales efforts. *Courtesy CBS Television Network.*

pected letterhead, it almost carries the publication's endorsement.

Seventeen Magazine, among others, helps local retailers sponsor fashion shows using clothing featured in the magazine's ads
and editorial columns. In addition, as noted in Chapter 3, many
magazines have regional editions, which makes merchandising
a particular ad in a specific area even easier.

Many trade, business and professional magazines offer reader
inquiry service cards (Bingo Cards) on which a reader can circle
a number to get more information about the product advertised
in that issue. This service normally is free. Some of these publications will also feature the product you're advertising in that issue
in their editorial section without charge.

RETAIL AD MERCHANDISING

Local retailers can merchandise their advertising investment
by posting tear sheets of print ads in the store for customers to
see while they are shopping. Some of these shoppers probably
never saw the ad when it originally appeared. Also, a copy of
the ad should be delivered to the department in which the item
is being sold so that sales personnel are familiar with the special
features. Likewise, this ad should be posted at the check-out area
in drug and variety stores and near the switchboard operators
who handle telephone orders.

Use of the in-store public address system can easily supplement in-store posting of these special advertised values. Tying-
in with other available communication opportunities in a retail
store to help merchandise the paid media advertising was discussed in Chapter 9.

It's worth noting that local media themselves heavily merchandise the use of advertising to get local retailers interested
in special sections and supplements that usually tie into a season
or holiday. When an advertiser buys space in this special section,
the newspaper will often supply him with such items as window
posters, stickers and tags that announce "Big Sell-A-Bration, as
advertised in the Daily Press."

WHOSE JOB?

In a corporation most of the planning for the merchandising
of advertising is done by the manufacturer's advertising depart-

Seven extra-special Sundays in 1982

New York Times Magazine editors are already looking, touching, watching, questioning, listening, tasting, sniffing, noting and gathering the news — for seven wonderful Part 2s of the Times Magazine to be published in 1982 for your particular enjoyment.

WOMEN'S FASHIONS OF THE TIMES
March 7 and August 29

MEN'S FASHIONS
March 28 and September 12

HOME DESIGN
April 18 and September 26

HOME ENTERTAINING
October 24

Note to advertisers: If you'd like information about rates and closing dates, please call Philip Du Val, Marketing Director THE NEW YORK TIMES MAGAZINE (212) 556-1203

SELF-MERCHANDISING: A medium will often promote itself by pointing out specific opportunities it offers advertisers. © 1982 by The New York Times Company. Reprinted by permission.

ment. Rarely does the advertising agency get into the act. Why? First, it costs money. In the absence of media commissions, an agency would be compensated on a special fee basis, which could be expensive. Second, the manufacturer's ad staff is close to the center of things—close to the sales department, the manufacturing operation and other groups that have roles in merchandising programs. In the home office the copywriter can strike fast by virtue of being ideally located to orchestrate ad merchandising programs.

Merchandising of advertising is necessary because you've learned never to take it for granted that those people whom you want to see your ad have actually seen it. You're protecting yourself and your company's investment by merchandising your advertising to your own dealers, to your own sales reps and to those other people important to the success of your campaign. You've invested too much to let an ad appear and let it go at that. You can never tell people too often what you want them to hear!

Copy
research

11

Unfortunately, research is a scare word among many advertising copywriters. Why? Mainly because it's misunderstood. Writers too often view research as an encroachment on their territory. They see research people as a bunch of technicians with sheaves of charts and tables who claim to have all the answers necessary to develop the most effective advertising.

Perhaps it's merely a modern manifestation of the old Art versus Science argument that's been hovering around for centuries. Writers feel that their creative skills are being replaced by numerical conclusions that may differ from their own. The researcher has no such sinister intention at all and merely seeks to give the writer a more accurate and up-to-date definition of the market to which the advertising is being addressed.

The biggest mistake made by research people is to present each report as gospel. It's not. The biggest mistake made by writers is to reject by reflex any research that conflicts with their own instincts. That's arrogance. And in the advertising business there's room for neither dogma nor arrogance.

LIVING WITH RESEARCH

Writers and researchers should work hand in hand. Good writers are grateful for any help research can provide. Good research people see their studies as an essential support service that is in no way a substitute for the creative contribution by the writer. When this kind of rapport is established, the results will be very fruitful, certainly a goal to strive for.

The level of research activity you can expect swings from one extreme to the other, depending on where you write. Advertising agencies generally offer the most complete research facilities. They're equipped to initiate market studies (to guide the initial creative development) and post-test procedures (to determine whether established objectives were reached). Research on this scale, interpreted cautiously, should be greeted enthusiastically by the copywriter.

Many corporations also provide extensive research for use by their own advertising departments and, hopefully, for transmittal to their advertising agencies. Manufacturers must necessarily maintain ongoing studies of their markets so that they are alerted to any shifting winds far enough in advance to do something about them. In the course of conducting these surveys, a wealth of data is mined that can be put to good use by those responsible for the preparation of advertising. What often happens, in fact, is that this research dovetails with agency research projects, avoiding duplication.

Retail advertisers often have available to them the least basic research. This means copywriters who write retail ads are heavily dependent on their instincts and their experience. Some guidance can be obtained from various industry associations if the retailer is a member. These associations have been formed to represent virtually all groups, from dry cleaners to securities dealers. Their avowed purpose is to develop and coordinate promotions that will serve the interests of their sponsors. So naturally, their efforts are aimed toward studying the market to determine the most advantageous ways to present their products or services. Sophisticated research techniques for measuring the results of advertising are usually not needed at the retail level—you can tell quickly enough by the ringing of the cash register.

MARKET STUDIES

It seems almost unnecessary to say that a writer must know what he or she is talking about. (But doesn't some advertising you see make you wonder?) Much of this knowledge will be the accumulation of experience. Often you will have written ads before for the particular product or for other similar products so that what you learned was transferable. While there's no substitute for this kind of experience and for the insights and judgments it permits, current market data is essential.

The purpose of market research is to keep continuous tabs on the target audience. Needs shift. Attitudes vary. Styles change. What was red hot last year might be ice cold today. Innovations by your competition—either in the product itself or in the merchandising of it—might dictate a new strategy to maintain market share. A market is not monolithic. It's not stable and unmoving. It's in a constant state of flux, and wise marketers keep their ears pressed to the ground. Their very survival depends on staying alert to today's breezes that could be tomorrow's tornadoes.

Designing the market survey

If you get a chance to contribute to the design of a survey, leap at it. Let the research person know what you're trying to find out. Let him or her share your hunches so that the questionnaire can be constructed to validate them or eliminate them. Questions must always be phrased to neutralize any bias on the part of respondents, which is not always as easy as it sounds. As a writer, you won't become involved with the intricacies of designing the survey. Nor will you select the sample. These are professional tasks for specialists. It's enough to know that these factors can be crucial to the results.

The survey is basically concerned with such questions as the following:

- Who buys the product? (Very specific profile of your typical customer.)

- Why do they prefer the product? (Taste? Size? Convenience? Price? Or what?)

• What are the product's strengths and weaknesses? (Listen carefully, even if it hurts.)

• What can you learn from the competition? (You can be sure they're monitoring *you* just as well!)

Most of the time research findings will confirm what an experienced writer already believes to be true. Sometimes, though, a study will reveal a fact of explosive market potential, which happened when a market study once showed that 80% of the beer bought by New Yorkers was consumed by 20% of the people. In other words, the market was highly concentrated—those who drank beer, drank a lot of beer. The advertising response zeroed in on this tight market with classic directness: it became "The one beer to have when you're having more than one." The refrain ran for a dozen years or so and carried the brand to the top. There was no way the campaign could have been created without the research to define the precise nature of the audience.

Judging research results

When the time comes—and it will—when the research results come to a conclusion that varies from your own, be skeptical. Question it. Debate it. Perhaps even have it redone. This is not just a streak of stubbornness or writer's temperament but plain, hard-nosed good sense. Research is not a replacement for experience, insight or judgment. When you know the product and the market, your "gut feeling" should tell you about the thrust your advertising should take. These are the skills for which there is no substitute. When a survey contradicts all of this, doublecheck the survey.

This all calls for a certain amount of honesty and candor with yourself because there will be times when the research will indeed lead down new paths. Accept this with grace that is at least equal to the tenacity you demonstrated in questioning the research. Chalk it up to the learning process. Research that is conducted simply to certify your preconceived feelings is no research at all.

Once the creative work has started and a concept has been arrived at, how can you be sure you're on the right track? There's not an advertiser in the world who doesn't feel pangs of doubt at this point. The advertising is the synthesis of your experience, the available research and the creative skills that finally breathe a spark of life into the avalanche of facts and figures from various sources.

There's no certification that's completely foolproof. If you're looking for absolutes, forget it. Advertising isn't mathematics or chemistry. It's subjective, not scientific, even though "it can be planned somewhat scientifically," in the words of the late Paul M. Lund, former vice president of American Telephone and Telegraph Company. The very best you can hope for is some small signal that your efforts are triggering the desired response. Ultimately, the final decision will hinge on judgment, intuition and experience, as always. Still, there is much to be gained by making this effort to measure people's reaction to creative concepts before a total commitment (financial as well as emotional) is made.

There are a number of methods to accomplish this in some small measure. In fact, there are probably dozens of ways (or more) because most manufacturers have their own pet research techniques for testing the market, the acceptability of their products and the effectiveness of their advertising. This is especially true for packaged goods, whose life span is extremely short, often just a few years. There is scant room for error. Profitability must be achieved quickly. Constant research is the only way to avoid a costly bath in red ink.

PRE-TESTING TECHNIQUES

The most common techniques for pre-testing advertising ideas can be grouped into three broad categories: group evaluation, individual reaction and measured response to alternate executions. Maybe that sounds like too much jargon, but as you'll see, they're really very basic approaches to a very ticklish problem: how to pry people's real thoughts out of their heads. That done, then devise some way to judge objectively what they said. There's a big difference between what people say and what they mean. Not because they mean to be deceptive, but because the research environment is intrinsically artificial. People in this situation immediately start to act like judges and not like consumers.

They watch their words and guard their reactions. They want to be thought of as intelligent and sophisticated. They become less than candid without knowing it. The raw data drawn from this research must be interpreted carefully. That's when a good research person needs special skills.

Focus groups

One procedure of group evaluation is the Focus Group. This is a gathering of people with generally the same characteristics (sex, age, income level) as the target audience. Normally about a dozen are in a group. Coffee and snacks are often served. Sometimes lunch. Every effort is made to make the participants relax so they won't hold back once the program gets underway. The entire session—averaging two hours—is put on tape for later transcription and study. (You'd be surprised how easy it is to overlook some chance remark in the flurry of activity!) The group leader is a trained professional who is thoroughly familiar with the product, the strategy and the objective of the advertising, and who guides the discussion in a direction that will draw out candid opinions on the subject.

As the group warms up, a skilled leader can transform a circle of strangers into a friendly coffee klatch, with obviously beneficial results. At the start, the group doesn't know why they're assembled, except in the most general terms. ("We're going to talk about hair shampoo. Are you willing to sit in this group and discuss this subject?") After the people get accustomed to each other and grow familiar with the surroundings, they are introduced to whatever specific material is involved. It could be in the form of "concept boards" that simply indicate a possible claim for the product (for example, "The First Soft Shampoo"). Or they could be shown actual ad layouts, with or without the copy set in type. They invariably volunteer their opinions (sometimes there's no holding them back!). But it's vital to be able to sort out their responses as "judges" from their responses as "consumers." It's a distinction that must be made if you're to attach any validity at all to the expressed opinions.

While the observations made by participants must be weighed with great caution, it's possible to gain useful insights into the way people think about your product. Often what's unsaid is as meaningful as what's said. And sometimes real surprises pop up. Consider this reaction by a young woman when shown a simple but innovative new way to apply antiperspirant. She said, "I don't believe it can be done that way because if it could it would have been already." Don't laugh. There's a lesson about the thought processes of the customers to whom you're trying to appeal. Deep down many people are comfortable with the old and familiar and are very reluctant to adopt the new and imaginative. But if Thomas Edison and Orville Wright weren't disturbed by this kind of discouragement, why should you be?

Maybe this resistance is not typical, but it is fresh evidence that odd obstacles often stand between getting those consumers to notice your product and convincing them to take it home. Fair warning for every copywriter: don't take anything for granted. The stubborn streak that demands, "Prove it!" is more prevalent than you'd like to think. Imagine yourself talking to the most obstinate prospect possible. Write as if to win over this one person and you'll catch many of the easier prospects in your net.

Although Focus Groups can provide useful insights about human behavior, naturally they're not perfect. The sample used, for instance, could be unrepresentative. An outspoken participant can cow the others into agreement—or, even worse, into silence. The leader can fail to probe properly or to follow up with gusto. But normally this kind of research can be very helpful—just as long as you understand that it's only providing guidance and is not supplying solutions. In the end it's up to you, as usual.

One final note about Focus Groups. The group is frequently being observed by interested parties through a oneway mirror. Many agencies have facilities like this (often called "fish bowls," for obvious reasons), as do private research organizations and college psychology departments. The reason for this outside group of observers is simple: seeing people's reactions can be as important as hearing their remarks. If this strikes you as an intrusion of privacy, you should also know that the best group leaders frequently insist that this fact be made known to the group. Then they, remarkably, put the group at ease about it. You'd be surprised how quickly the participants ignore the mirror and the invisible audience and get down to brass tacks!

Individual reaction

Probably the most widespread method of evaluating advertising is done on a one-to-one basis. Here a single interviewer confronts a single respondent, who is shown one or more ads and then asked questions. The interviewer records the reactions in a way that can be measured and interpreted later. Well-designed tests of this nature concentrate the testing among those considered the likeliest prospects. Obviously, testing an ad for a farm implement would take place in an agricultural community. But the focus must be sharpened even more: to dairy farmers or wheat farmers or whatever, depending on the specific machine in the ad being tested. For certain types of products, ZIP codes are a helpful guide to pinpoint an audience by income as well as geography. The important thing is to try to expose the ad to those in your target group. Otherwise, the evaluation is worthless.

The interviewer shows the test ad to a respondent. After a suitable time, the material is returned to the interviewer, who proceeds to ask questions according to a very structured formula that's compatible for both computer and manual tabulation. How much information can the respondent remember? Is this the principal benefit or is the respondent missing the point? Is the claim believable? The questions may vary but the objective always remains the same: does the ad perform as well in the field as it promised back in the office?

The ad being tested is sometimes included in a magazine format (usually "dummied" into a real or mock-up magazine), so the respondent is faced with competition for her or his attention, just as in the real world. This reveals how well the ad does its job. When the test ad is simply handed to the respondent, obviously there's no way to judge its ability to draw attention away from competing ads. Still, this latter method of pre-testing has strong adherents because of its value in determining if your general thrust is of interest to the subject and is presented in a credible fashion. You should know that a certain percentage of every test group can be counted on to say, "No, I don't believe it because I don't believe anything they say in the ads." Alas, we all must bear this heavy burden.

Any number of variations are available. Frequently, an open-ended question is included to give the respondent an opportunity to add verbatim comments. Even though these off-the-cuff comments may not be included in the tabulated results, you should study them carefully for any clues. Sometimes a respondent expresses thoughts that don't emerge in the formal question period. Don't leave any stone unturned. Use all the input you are fortunate enough to get your hands on.

Alternate executions

There will be times when you want to determine which of two different variations of a given ad is more effective. The most common method of accomplishing this is the "split run" (see p. 126). Many publications are able to print one version in half the copies of a certain issue and the other version in the identical spot in the remaining copies. Each ad should have a coupon containing a "key" number or letter for identification. When the mail comes in, you simply count how many returns came from each version.

It's important that there be only one variable in each test ad. When the results come in, you want to be able to determine why one pulled better than the other, and to do this you have to be able to isolate the difference. Ideally, you should test different headlines (benefits) with the same illustrations, or different illustrations with the same headline—just as long as you are able to pinpoint exactly what it is that accounts for the performance of one ad versus another. Not all publications can offer split runs. There is normally a small surcharge for this service. But it's well worth it.

POST-TESTING ADS

Naturally, it's in the interest of advertisers to seek ways to measure the effectiveness of a single ad or commercial. Is the ad read? Is the commercial seen? Does the promise stimulate the desired response? Big budgets ride on decisions of this sort. How can you get the answers?

The most widely recognized and generally accepted service for this purpose is the Daniel Starch organization. A sample of people who have read the magazine being tested are afterward quizzed in depth about what they have read. The survey is conducted shortly after the person can be expected to have completed the magazine. An interviewer then arrives and flips through the pages in the presence of this respondent, asking whether he or she remembers seeing each ad at all.

Further questions are asked about each element in the ad: headline, illustration, text, caption, logo. The result is a very definitive score for each area of the ad. The ad as a whole, along with each individual section, is then assigned a percentage rating which can be compared to the scores of all the other ads in the magazine. Ratings are grouped as follows: *Noted* (respondent remembers seeing the ad), *Associated* (respondent is able to identify the ad with the name of the brand or advertiser), and *Read Most* (respondent has read half or more than half the words in the copy).

With this data, and knowing the cost for each ad in the magazine, Starch is also able to assign a cost-efficiency ratio to each ad. In other words, a small black-and-white ad (low cost) might be more efficient than a four-color bleed ad (high cost) based on the number of people who saw the ad. Even if more people saw the color ad, it might not have been a sufficient number to justify the extra cost.

Because Starch reports have been issued for so many years, a large body of norms has been assembled as guidelines. But they are just that—guides. Even though Starch might not be able to "prove" statistically that headlines on top of the illustration are more effective than underneath, for example, please don't take it as dogma. Intuition and ingenuity are at the heart of all successful ads. The minute everybody begins to follow the same "rules," a deadly parity is reached. Accept guidance, but then do your own thing. Remember, according to accepted aerodynamic principles, the bumblebee can't fly. The copywriter's job is to design more bumblebees.

POST-TESTING COMMERCIALS

There are a number of different testing procedures currently in favor. Most are based on a telephone survey of several hundred homes on the day after the test commercial aired. Respondents are asked, first of all, whether they recall seeing the commercial. If so, they are checked further for message playback. On the plus side, this kind of test provides a quick "score" of the commercial in a real-life situation. But even so, the results are apt to be misleading since responses are seldom confined to the specific target audience. The ultimate test, of course, is the cash register. But advertisers want to know whether or not a commercial "works" before they throw their full weight behind it.

TEST MARKETS

Probably the most common method of testing whether or not a commercial is working is putting it on the air in a test market. That is, airing it in a single city and carefully monitoring the results. If it's a new product, the manufacturer makes certain to control all the other variables that may affect purchasing— availability, price, competitive pressure—so that the advertising element can be isolated and its effectiveness measured. For a known product, the new commercial can be shown in a test area, only this time the results are measured against a predetermined comparable period. While the effort to "prove" whether a commercial measures up to expectations is seldom completely conclusive, it does provide some basic guidance.

As renowned an advertising man as David Ogilvy has said, "The most important word in the vocabulary of advertising is *test*." Asking, watching, observing, measuring—these are integral ingredients in creating copy that sells. But don't expect miracles. Research simply won't relieve you of the final responsibility of weighing the evidence and following your instincts.

SOME PRECAUTIONS

Nobody's ever invented a better barometer than the cash register. But there's a good chance the ads or commercials you're writing are several steps removed from the marketplace. They can't be gauged with such beautiful simplicity, nor so readily. Even if you've analyzed the market situation and positioned your product properly and even if you've tested the execution and are satisfied that it conveys the benefit convincingly, the only way you'll know it's all working is when it's in the magazines or on the air. Before this it's all a laboratory exercise despite every effort to simulate the actual consumer environment.

Selling the product is, of course, the ultimate objective. A number of other marketing factors always enter the scene and prevent any clear appraisal of the advertising itself. A prospect may see your message and be persuaded to buy the product but may then fail to find it in the store. (How can you fault the advertising for that?) Or a prospect might go out to buy and be turned off by the price tag. (A marketing problem that advertising can't always be expected to overcome.) Or your prospect is faced with a flurry of competitive activity in the form of coupons, savings, and other deals of this type. (How can advertising anticipate the defensive tactics of the other brands in the field?)

If an observer were standing by and simply tallying sales during the period of advertising, ignoring the other influences on the market, you can see how misleading such conclusions are likely to be. The advertising might very well be labeled "unsuccessful" when in fact it performed very nicely, only to be let down by others in the marketing process. Advertising is only one element in the marketing mix, but because it's the most visible one, it gets much more attention—both good and bad—than it probably deserves. Learn to live with this fact of life.

The following are some hard questions to ask yourself about research:

- Was the sample used (number of respondents) big enough?

- Was it a truly random sample or a sample in which other factors were operating, such as telephone ownership or home ownership?

- Were the people interviewed directly involved in the problem or its solution?

- Was the sample representative?

- Did the sample correspond to your target audience? What's the point of interviewing women over 45 if the product's best potential customers are known to be young mothers?

Beyond mere percentages, look for the actual number of respondents. A "50% in favor" result is far less impressive if you learn that only two people were interviewed and one agreed and the other disagreed!

As a copywriter, you should try to remember these points about the research put at your disposal:

- Don't expect research to make hard decisions for you. Maybe it can narrow the range, but the final choice is squarely up to you.

- Don't use research as a security blanket. Successful advertising is the only thing that warms a good writer.

- Don't let research findings inhibit your creative instincts, what the late Leo Burnett called your "wee small voice." Numbers will never replace ideas in advertising.

Production
pitfalls

12

A copywriter's primary mission is, of course, creating the advertising. But how do assignments start? Who gives the orders? What about photography? Artwork? Typesetting? A host of activities take place within your organization that relate to internal control of work in progress and to the actual physical production of the advertising you've written. A copywriter must know more about the business than just putting one word after the other.

Each company or agency will have its own system of procedures, but some of the more fundamental considerations are covered here. Just as you must become involved with research and sales representatives at the information-gathering stage, now you must become familiar with some of the nitty-gritty details that are necessary for your advertising to get beyond the sheet-of-paper-in-the-typewriter stage.

There are plenty of pitfalls waiting for the unwary copywriter. The more you're able to anticipate them, and therefore avoid them, the easier your job will be.

COMMUNICATION

The best advice is *always get it in writing*. The order that authorizes work to begin—get it in writing. The schedule for shooting photographs of the new model or new merchandise—get it in writing. Any change in scheduling—get it in writing.

Every phone call you make that involves new, revised or deleted instructions—follow it up with a memo. Later, if there are missed deadlines and an investigation by supervisors, you'll at least know what you said and when. Be particularly careful if you're working for a small organization and have direct contact with suppliers: printers, model agencies, photographers or direct-mail houses, where there are more chances for slip-ups for which you're personally responsible. Put it in writing and file it. Someday it could help find who's responsible if something goes wrong.

Never part with your only copy of anything you write. Be sure to keep a carbon or photocopy. Production personnel (even artists) have been known to misplace copy just before a deadline. Then you're stuck with starting from scratch and getting approvals all over again. After it happens once, you'll never part with your original and only piece of copy again!

Rarely does a copywriter have the pleasure of approving his or her own copy. Usually you're writing for someone who will approve your copy before it goes to production. Often this approval requirement involves half a dozen people. Be the biggest initials-collector around. If others must have a say about your work, be sure you ask them to put their approving initials on the copy or layout so that later they can't say that what you did wasn't what they wanted. All in all, it saves headaches later. Before people sign, they usually think twice, so your dogged pursuit of initials saves a lot of casual OKs.

Also, get a layout for every job you do no matter how simple it is. An artist and a copywriter are two creative people. Sometimes they talk alike but visualize differently. Take no chances. Even if it's a simple job like a business card, get a layout.

TYPESETTING

You should be aware of what your copy will look like after it's set in type. An artist or art director will play a key role here.

But it's a good idea for you to have a "feel" for type selection and type size so that you can make sure your ad looks like what you had in mind when you wrote it. The following are some tips about type you might find useful:

- If your copy is long, break it up with boldface subheads or short boldface paragraphs. Extra white space between paragraphs also will help readability and attractiveness and will invite the reader's eye to continue down the column. You can also intersperse small graphics throughout the copy, but not if they make the ad look "spotty."

- Copy set in very narrow columns often has so many hyphens it's difficult to read. Avoid narrow column widths. Why make things difficult for your readers?

- Beware of setting your copy in very long lines. Tests have shown that readers tend to reject excessively wide columns of type. It's hard for the eye to follow long lines. As a general rule, the wider the column the larger the type should be.

- If your copy will appear in reverse (white on black or any other color), be sure the type is large enough. Type appears smaller when it's reversed, so just because it appears satisfactory in black on white, don't presume it will be the same when reversed.

- Reject "squint-size" type in any ad. Don't normally accept text-size type smaller than 10 points with 2 points of leading (space) between the lines. This book is set in 10 point type; headings are 13 points, chapter titles are 36 points.

- Normally you don't spec the type. You don't fit the text blocks. You have enough to do to conceive the ad, write it, help select graphics for it and keep it on schedule. Still, it's advisable to have a working knowledge of the subject, if only to be able to make your meaning clear to those who are working along with you.

PASTE-UPS

After the type is set and approved, it is then placed in proper position on the layout along with any illustrations and the logo.

The result is called a "mechanical." It's really nothing more than a very accurate paste-up. At this stage, you get a good idea of what your ad will finally look like when it's printed.

Make a point to check the mechanical very carefully before it goes to the printer. Take your time. Try not to be rushed. An extra glance may save you hours or days. Sometimes the paste-up artist will space the type a little differently than what you or the original layout artist visualized. This improper spacing can often happen in the headline, making it difficult to read. Or maybe a line will be broken oddly, causing the thought pattern of your message to get jumbled. Or you may have an ad with punctuation sticking out in strange places! This is the stage when you can really polish your ad to a professional finish.

Now that you can see what your ad will look like, you should be prepared to resist any proposal to reduce this mechanical to a smaller size. Well-intentioned people may suggest that, for example, a standard newspaper-page-size ad be reduced to a tabloid-page size. This would save money (no need to reset type or make a new mechanical) but the result would not be worth the saving. Remember, *everything* goes down in size, not just the headlines and illustrations—the text type itself often shrinks to squint-size or worse.

ILLUSTRATIONS

Not all artwork is suitable in all printed media. Magazines are usually printed on slick, coated stock (paper), which provides top-quality reproduction of just about anything. But newspapers, on the other hand, are printed on much coarser stock (newsprint), which cannot give the same kind of reproduction. For one thing, halftones (the gradations of gray you get in photographs) don't reproduce as well in newspapers as they do in magazines. If you must use photos, make sure the message isn't dependent on small details in the photo because these may not come out clearly. Or you might want to consider some method of converting the photographs to line art (which has no gradations of gray), which reproduces better in newspapers. A variety of technical processes are available for this purpose. Or you might even want to switch to drawn artwork, making sure the artist is instructed that the illustration is for newspapers.

Before a photographer goes on an assignment, brief him or her thoroughly. Of course the photographer knows better than you the right film, camera settings and other photographic techniques. But he or she may not have the same perception as you about the job. Sometimes you'll want the photographer to shoot for a certain effect that hasn't been (or can't be) portrayed in the layout, or the photographer may find a location shot you couldn't possibly anticipate. Photographers are creative people and can often make a genuine contribution to the ad.

Usually try to avoid using photographs that are straight, head-on shots. Specify angles. Have the photographer shoot from above or from below as long as there's no misleading distortion. In this way you'll usually get a more interesting shot.

More sophisticated organizations ask the photographer to "shoot to the layout." In this way he or she gets the model or the product at the proper angle to fit the layout as you and the artist have visualized it. The photographer actually goes to the job with a rough layout to shoot from.

Try to avoid photos with busy or cluttered backgrounds. It may be pretty, but does it sell? The whole idea is to draw attention to the product benefit embodied in the photograph. There's no place for anything that distracts from this.

PRINTING

You may or may not work directly with printers, but you should have some appreciation of what they can do for you. They are experts in their own field—printing, stock, reproduction methods and binding.

See the proof for all your jobs. Insist on it. Otherwise how do you know what you're getting? It's better to lose a little time and get it right than to have 100,000 copies that are printed wrong. No matter how simple or how small the job, always insist on a printer's proof. Then see a corrected proof for all your jobs that needed correction. Get it the way you want it and get it right, for yourself and your client.

Refuse colors that don't print the way you want them. Color correction is possible. Be sure to see a color proof for all printed jobs. Magenta (a purplish red color) is a particular problem, but it can be corrected to the shade you want. Check color registration (alignment). If colors don't line up perfectly, you get a fuzzy, distorted picture.

If the printer is printing on an offset press, your copy should not look gray (unless that's the way you wanted it). Grayness is a printer's problem. Make him solve it.

Your copy should not bleed through the stock. This means you should not be able to see the ink on the reverse side of the paper. If you do, something was wrong with the printing solution (if offset press) or an inadequate stock was used.

For quality control you should inspect a delivered job at three places: take a sample from the top, the middle and the bottom. Quality control also involves the reaction of the sun on certain inks. Put a sample in a sunny window for a week or two if the ad material (such as POP) will be exposed to the sun in actual use.

Printers normally give quantity discounts, but don't fall into the trap of ordering more than you can reasonably expect to need.

Always make sure you instruct your printer to add the production number of the job in small type tucked in a corner at the bottom. You have no idea how this little step simplifies reordering.

If you're creating product spec sheets (specification sheets showing the product and its important details), avoid putting prices on them. Prices usually change more frequently than the company's models, styles or products, and so they should be printed on a separate "slip sheet" for your sales representatives or slipped into the printed catalog. Then when there's a price change, it's simple and quick to print a new, inexpensive price list rather than redo an entire spec sheet or catalog.

If you're getting heavily involved with a printer, be sure to visit the shop. Inspect the operation to see if you feel that your work can be handled, for it may be farmed out to another printer by your "printer."

In most sections of the country there are, invariably, a number of printers nearby who are qualified to do your work. It's a very competitive business. If one printer gets careless or lazy, there's always another waiting in the wings. Don't settle for merely adequate work when superior workmanship is never far away. And don't always settle for the lowest price when a job is open to competitive bids. Top-quality results come first, low prices second.

A copywriter's interest in printing is obvious: the finished product should be worthy of all the sweat you poured into creating it. If it's not, you'll rightly feel cheated. You should understand what to do—and what not to do—in order to get your ad produced to your satisfaction.

Postscript

By this time, we hope you feel a little more comfortable with "how advertising happens" and somewhat better equipped to start making a contribution. However, no book, no teacher, no course of study can ever provide more than the basic tools and, perhaps, a head start in the right direction. The rest is up to you. The three most important things you can do from now on are practice, practice and practice some more. Theory is important, to be sure—you won't progress very far unless you grasp it—but there's simply no substitute for getting out and doing it, putting into play the ideas presented on these pages.

You'll probably discover rather quickly that advertising is a popular field for those with a creative bent. In other words, it's crowded. You'll be up against some very bright people. How to make yourself stand out in the crowd? Never lose sight of the fact that advertising is a business; its goal is to get results. Impress on a prospective employer that you understand this—and are prepared to prove it—and suddenly you're the candidate who gets a second look. Certainly you've got to show flair and demon-

202

strate good taste and possess that elusive commodity called creativity. But above all you must always remember what advertising is all about: generating action that wouldn't have happened otherwise. Advertising is really very simple; it's only made unnecessarily complex by those who misunderstand its purpose.

Its purpose, however, is not always making something happen right now, today, this week. To be sure, most retail advertising displays this urgency with its heavy emphasis on prices and sales. But many companies use advertising to accomplish long-range objectives as well: to establish confidence in a brand name, for instance, or to reinforce a manufacturer's reputation for reliable products. These are often no less important to a corporation's marketing strategy than the response elicited by the cents-off coupon in tonight's newspaper.

The important point to remember is that advertising must sell, either now or at some distant point in time. It's not just an exercise in altruism. Even such noteworthy examples of "helpful" advertising as the "Come to Shell for Answers" booklets and the International Paper Company's "How to" series (How to Improve Your Vocabulary, How to Use the Library, et al.) will ultimately be judged on the way they affected each company's performance in the marketplace. Critical once again is the copywriter's skill in organizing ideas and words in a manner that will move people to action.

Advertising is all around us, more than ever. And remember, behind every ad there is a copywriter. The typical U.S. household watches television for more than six hours a day and all those commercials on view were spawned by copywriters. Think of all the newspapers and magazines that pass before your eyes every week, brimming with ads that came from copywriters. The truth is, the work of many advertising copywriters is probably more widely read than that of our best-selling authors. The first time you read your words in a national magazine, or hear them on your car radio or see them on your television screen is liable to be a heady experience. All at once, hundreds of thousands, or even millions, of people are exposed to your ideas! All your sweat is suddenly worth it. The surge of pride you feel is well earned.

Chances are, advertising in one form or another will continue to grow in economic importance far into the future. The more goods made, the more services offered, the greater the need for

KNOWING H
COULD DOUBL
OF AMERICA
DID YOU H

Business today is held together by its communication system. And listening is undoubtedly its weakest link.

Most of us spend about half our business hours listening. Listeni poorly. Research studies show that on the average we listen at a 25% level of efficiency.

A statistic that is not only surprisingly low, but terribly costly.

With more than 100 million workers in America, a simple ten dollar listening mistake by each of them would cost a billion dollars.

Letters have to be retyped; appointments rescheduled; shipments reshipped.

And when people in large corporations fail to listen to one anoth the results are even costlier.

ADVERTISING AT ITS BEST: This series from the Sperry Corporation exemplifies the power of the printed word, serving at once, both the company's ends and the common good. *Courtesy Sperry Corporation.*

TO LISTEN
HE EFFICIENCY
BUSINESS.
R THAT?

Ideas get distorted by as much as 80% as they travel through the
ieldy chain of command.

Employees feel more and more distant, and ultimately alienated
top management.

Well, as one of the world's largest corporations—with 87,000
loyees and five divisions—we at Sperry simply can't afford to pay the
e of poor listening.

So we've set up extensive listening programs that Sperry personnel
ughout the world can take part in. From sales representatives to
puter engineers to the Chairman of the Board.

These programs are making us a lot better at listening to each other.
when you do business with Sperry Univac, or
any of our other divisions, you'll discover that

they're making us a lot better at listening to you.

⊹ SPERRY

We understand how important it is to listen.

Sperry is Sperry Univac computers, Sperry New Holland farm equipment,
Sperry Vickers fluid powers systems, and guidance and control equipment
from Sperry division and Sperry Flight Systems.

How efficient a listener are you?
Write to Sperry, Dept. 4C, 1290 Avenue of the Americas, New York, New York 10019,
for a listening quiz that's both fun and a little surprising.

a medium to convey the message. All the more reason to remember that many people make decisions based on what you say to them. Don't misuse this trust. Shun the temptation to stretch the truth. Learn to level with your readers, to win them over with candor. Help them. Serve them. Show them you like them and maybe they'll return the favor by going out and doing what you're asking them to do. Because that, after all, is what copywriting is all about.

Helpful resources

The following list of information sources makes no pretense of being complete: it is more directional than definitive. A complete list would be too lengthy for inclusion here. The following addresses should, however, get you started. They should lead you to the reference source for any specific problem or question you may have. Omission of any name from this list is no indication of its relative importance.

PUBLICATIONS

Advertising Age
740 Rush Street
Chicago, IL 60611

Art Direction
10 East 39th Street—6th Floor
New York, NY 10016

Broadcasting
1735 De Sales Street, NW
Washington, DC 20036

Co-Op News
A SRDS Company
5201 Old Orchard Road
Skokie, IL 60077

DM (Direct Marketing) News
156 East 52nd Street
New York, NY 10022

Editor & Publisher
575 Lexington Avenue
New York, NY 10022

Marketing & Media Decisions
342 Madison Avenue
New York, NY 10017

TV/Radio Age
1270 Avenue of the Americas
New York, NY 10020

MEDIA ASSOCIATIONS

Cabletelevision Advertising Bureau
767 Third Avenue
New York, NY 10017

Direct Mail Marketing Association
6 East 43rd Street
New York, NY 10017

Institute Of Outdoor Advertising
485 Lexington Avenue
New York, NY 10017

Magazine Publishers Association
575 Lexington Avenue
New York, NY 10022

National Cable TV Association
1724 Massachusetts Avenue, NW
Washington, DC 20036

Newspaper Advertising Bureau
485 Lexington Avenue
New York, NY 10017

The Newspaper Center
Box 17407
Dulles International Airport
Washington, DC 20041

Point of Purchase Advertising Institute
60 East 42nd Street
New York, NY 10165

Premium Advertising Association
420 Lexington Avenue
New York, NY 10017

Radio Advertising Bureau
485 Lexington Avenue
New York, NY 10017

Specialty Advertising Association
740 North Rush Street
Chicago, IL 60611

Television Bureau of Advertising
485 Lexington Avenue
New York, NY 10017

RESEARCH ORGANIZATIONS

A.C. Nielsen Company
1290 Avenue of the Americas
New York, NY 10019

Advertising Research Foundation
3 East 54th Street
New York, NY 10022

American Research Bureau
4320 Ammendale Road
Beltsville, MD 20705

Arbitron
1350 Avenue of the Americas
New York, NY 10019

Gallup & Robinson, Inc.
575 Ewing Street, PO Box 525
Princeton, NJ 08540

Starch/INRA/Hooper
566 East Boston Post Road
Mamaroneck, NY 10543

MISCELLANEOUS

Advertising Checking Bureau
2 Park Avenue
New York, NY 10016

American Association of Advertising Agencies
200 Park Avenue
New York, NY 10017

Association of National Advertisers
155 East 44th Street
New York, NY 10017

Audit Bureau of Circulations
123 North Wacker Drive
Chicago, IL 60606

Ayer Directory of Publications
Ayer Press
One Bala Avenue
Bala-Cynwyd, PA 19004

Institute of Canadian Advertising
8 King Street East
Toronto, Ontario M5C 1B5
Canada

Standard Directory of Advertising Agencies
The National Register Publishing Co.
5201 Old Orchard Road
Skokie, IL 60077

Standard Rate & Data Service
5201 Old Orchard Road
Skokie, IL 60077

Index

Account executives, 6, 8
Action, in copywriting formula,
     76–77
Advertisements
   elements in, 89
   composition of. *See* Copywriting
   placement of, 29–31, 40–41
   post-testing of, 190–191
   reprints of, 177
Advertising
   deceptive, 23–24
   defense of, 22–23
   directories for, 50–51
   marketing relations to, 17–18
   media selection in, 25–26, 59
      efficiency measures for, 26–28
      for local advertisers, 28
      magazine, 37
      newspaper, 28–29
      outdoor advertising, 44–45
      radio, 35

Advertising (*Continued*)
      television, 36
      time factor in, 65
   merchandising of, 169–181
      for co-op advertising, 173–177
      for dealer support, 171–173
      manufacturer staff in, 179–181
      media assistance in, 177–179
      through retail display, 179
      to sales personnel, 170–171
   merchandising relations to, 18
   production pitfalls in, 195–207
   public relations and, 19
   on specialty items, 50
   team effort in, 5
   See also specific type
Advertising agencies, 6–14
   account executive role in, 6
   in campaign planning, 164
   client relations with, 8, 13–14
   compensation to, 10–11

Advertising agencies (*Continued*)
　for basic service, 12
　for extra service, 12
　local rates in, 11–12
　copywriter function in, 1–2, 12
　one-person organization, 16–17
　operating procedures in, 8–10
　organizational network in, 6–8
　research facilities in, 183
　selection of, 13
Advertising campaigns, 147–168
　for company promotion, 151–
　　153
　competition in, 48
　coordination and continuity in,
　　149–150
　duration of, 164–166
　in flights, 166–167
　institutional, 153–156
　local follow-up to, 167
　for national brands, 150–151
　non-campaign ads and, 167–168
　objectives of, 148–149
　product differences in, 160
　product quality and, 149
　retail, 156–159
　slogans in, 158, 160–161
　unstated themes of, 161–162
　utility of, 147–148
Advertising Council, 156
AIDA (attention-interest-desire-
　action) formula, 75–76, 130
American Association of
　Advertising Agencies, 13
Art. *See* Illustration
Art director, 21, 94
Artist, 21, 94, 112
Art of Plain Talk, The (Flesch), 83,
　85
Associations, institutional
　advertising by, 156
Attention, in copywriting formula,
　75
Audience
　boredom barrier in, 58
　motivation of, 71, 74–75
　needs of, 59–61

Audience (*Continued*)
　psychological set of, 65
　target, 53–55
　television, 141
　for transit advertising, 50
Ayer Directory of Publications, 29

Balance, as design element, 108,
　109(fig.)
Billboards. *See* Outdoor
　advertising
Bingo cards, 179
Body copy, in print ad, 89
Brand loyalty, 57
Brand names, in national
　campaign, 150–151
Broadcast media. *See* Radio
　advertising; Television
　advertising
Burnett, Leo, 194
Business publications, 42, 179
Business reply mail, 122, 123(fig.)

Camera use, in television
　commercials, 138–141
Campaigns. *See* Advertising
　campaigns
Caption, 89, 98
Car cards, 50
Casket & Sunnyside (C&S), 42
Checkerboard position, 41
Circulars, 34
Clarity, in copywriting style, 79–80
Classified newspaper advertising,
　33–34
Cliches, 81
Clients
　advertising benefits to, 13–14
　agency contacts with, 6, 8
　agency selection by, 13
　presentations to, 8–10, 21–22
Clip art, 99(fig.), 110–112
Color
　correction of, 199–200
　in magazine advertising, 41–42
　in newspaper advertising, 33
Commercials, radio. *See* Radio spot

Commercials, television
  form for, 141–143
  length of, 138
  post-testing of, 191–192
Commission, agency, 10–12
Communications
  internal, 90–91
  as product pitfall, 196
Company promotions
  to demographic groups, 151–152
  service campaigns in, 152–153
  See also Institutional advertising
Competition, in advertising
    campaigns, 23, 148–149
Cooperative Advertising
    Agreements, 173–177
Copy Platform, 162
Copy Proposition, 162–163
Copyreading symbols, 85
Copy research, 55, 182–194
  evaluation of, 192–194
  levels of, 183
  market studies, 184–186
  post-testing in, 190–192
  pre-testing in, 186–190
  test markets for, 192
Copy sheet, 90, 91
  corrections on, 94
  coupon on, 126
  entries on, 92
  keyed, 100(fig.), 101, 115,
    117(fig.)
  physical requirements for, 92–
    94, 103
Copy Strategy, 163
Copywriter
  approving authority for, 91, 196
  artist relations with, 21
  client relations with, 8, 21–22
  design ability of, 96, 98, 103, 105
  function of, 1–2
  internal communication by, 90–
    91
  qualities of, 3
  research staff relations with,
    182–183, 194
  responsibilities of, 2

Copywriting
  ad simplicity in, 76–77
  in advertising agency, 12
  audience needs in, 59–61
  for broadcast media, 130–146
  common sense approach in, 56–
    57
  for direct mail advertising, 47–
    49, 121–125
  formula for, 75–76
  for magazine advertising, 115–
    121
  for magazine mail order, 125–
    128
  for newspaper advertising, 113–
    115
    ad department assistance with,
      15–16
  for noncampaign ads, 167–168
  for outdoor advertising, 128–129
  for point-of-purchase displays, 44
  positive emphasis in, 77–78
  preliminary steps to, 3–4, 52–53
  for print media, 113–129
  print techniques in. *See* Print
    techniques
  on product benefits, 58–59. *See
    also* Unique Selling
    Proposition (USP)
  production pitfalls in, 195–201
  for radio advertising, 131–137
  research for, 55, 56, 57–58. *See
    also* Copy research
  in retail advertising, 14–15, 158–
    159, 183
    for Co-op Agreement, 175
  style in, 79–85
    choppiness of, 82
    clarity of, 79–80
    correction symbols in, 85
    tips for, 80–81
    writing yardstick for, 83–85
  for target audience, 52–55
  for television advertising, 137–
    146
Corporate advertising. *See*
    Institutional advertising

Corporations
    ad merchandising in, 179–181
    in campaign planning, 164
    copywriter functions in, 1, 17
    employee morale in, 153, 156
    marketing director in, 17–18
    research by, 183
    See also Company promotion
Corrections
    color, 199–200
    copyreading symbols for, 85
    on copy sheet, 94
Coupons, mail order, 126
Covers, magazine advertisements
    on, 40
Creative Strategy, 163

Dealers
    campaign merchandising to,
        171–173
    trade advertising for, 67–70
Deceptive advertising, 23–24
Demographic groups
    company promotion to, 151–152
    magazine advertising for, 38
Department store. *See* Retail store
Design, 103–110
    balance in, 108, 109(fig.)
    copywriter role and, 103, 105
    dominant element in, 108, 110
    eyeflow in, 105–108
Desire, in copywriting formula, 76
Direct mail advertising
    addressing of, 122
    to build store traffic, 124–125
    copywriting for, 47–49, 122–125
    envelope in, 121–122, 125
    gimmick use in, 123–124
    mailing list for, 46, 49
    multiple mailings in, 124
    problems with, 125
Directories, advertising, 50–51
Direct Response advertising, 121
Display ads, 29
    classified, 33
Dolly shot, 140

Dominance, as design element,
    108, 110
Doodle layout, 94–96

Employee morale, institutional
    advertising for, 153, 156
End cards, 50
Envelope, in direct mail, 121–122,
    125
Eyeflow, as design element, 105–
    108

Film, *vs* tape, 143, 146
Fish bowls, for group observation,
    188
Flesch, Rudolf, 83–85
Flexiform, 31–33, 41
Flights, advertising campaigns in,
    166–167
Flip-flop boards, 45
Focus group, pre-testing of, 187–
    188
Franchises
    ad campaign coordination for,
        149
    ad inserts for, 34
Free lance specialists, 16–17

Gatefold, in magazine advertising,
    40
Gimmick use, in direct mail, 123–
    124
Group evaluation, in copy
    research, 187–188

Headline
    graphics for, 118
    in print ad, 89, 96, 107

Illustrations, 89, 98, 105
    clip art for, 110–112
    design of, 107
    product art for, 112
    production pitfalls in, 198–199
Image advertising. *See*
    Institutional advertising

Image-building, in retail campaign,
   158–159
Industrial publications, 179
   Unique Selling Proposition (USP)
      for, 70
Inserts, advertising, 34
Institute of Outdoor Advertising,
   45
Institutional advertising, 153–156
   by associations, 156
   motivation for, 153, 156
   public service, 156
Interest, in copywriting formula,
   76
Island magazine ad, 41

Keyed copy, 100(fig.), 102(fig.),
   101, 115, 117(fig.)

Layout. See Visual sheet
Logotype, in print ad, 89, 90, 96,
   108, 110
Lund, Paul M., 186

Magazine advertising, 37–42
   in business publications, 43
   color in, 41–43
   copywriting for, 115–121
   costs of, 37
   in demographic editions, 38
   lead time requirements in, 43
   magazine groupings and, 37
   mail order forms in, 125–128
   merchandising plans and, 177–
      179
   pass along readership and, 26
   preferred positions in, 40–41
   in regional editions, 38–40
   time factor in, 65, 118
   in unusual positions, 41
Mailing lists, purchase of, 46, 49
Mail order advertising, magazine,
   125–126
   coupons in, 126
   split-runs for, 126–128
   See also Direct mail advertising

Manufacturing corporations. See
   Corporations
Marketing
   advertising and, 17–18
   function of, 17
   product features for, 66
Market studies, 184–186
Media. See Advertising, media
   selection; specific type
Merchandising, 18. See also
   Advertising, merchandising
   of
Metro Associated Services (Metro),
   110
Multiple mailings, 124
Music
   in broadcast ads, 60–61
   campaign unity through, 148
   in radio advertising, 132–133,
      134
Musicians, pay scale for, 133

National advertising, Unique
   Selling Proposition (USP) in,
   61–66
Negatives, avoidance of, 77
Newspaper advertising, 28–34
   classified, 33–34
   color, 33
   copywriter role in, 27, 98
   copywriting for, 113–115
      by newspaper ad department,
      15–16
   display ads, 29
      in classified section, 33
   illustrations in, 198
      clip art, 110, 112
   morning-evening combination,
      28–29
   one-person organization for, 17
   placement criteria in, 29–31
   printed inserts in, 34
   printing problems in, 10
   rough layout in, 96–98
   in small spaces, 31–33
   total dollars spent on, 28
   in weeklies, 34

Omnibus ads, 115, 116(fig.),
117(fig.), 175
Outdoor advertising
copywriting for, 128–129
effectiveness of, 44, 45
locations for, 45
Outdoor Advertising Association of
America, 128

Pan shot, 139
Pass along readership, 26
Paste-ups, 197–198
Personal references, in ad copy, 85
Photography
production pitfalls of, 199
See also Illustrations
Point-of-purchase displays, 28, 42–
44
Postage-paid reply cards, 122,
123(fig.)
Post-testing
commercials, 191–192
print ads, 190–191
Present tense, 81
Pre-testing techniques
categories of, 186
by focus groups, 187–188
of individual reaction, 189–190
split run in, 190
Price, on print ad, 89, 98
Prime time advertising, 36, 37
Printing problems, 199–201
Print techniques
ad elements and, 88–90
for clip art, 110–112
for copy sheet, 92–94
design in, 103–110
for internal communications, 90–
91
keying, 100(fig.), 101, 102(fig.),
115, 117(fig.)
for visual sheet, 94–102
Production pitfalls, 195–201
communications as, 196
in illustrations, 198–199
in paste-ups, 197–198

Production pitfalls (Continued)
in printing, 199–201
in typesetting, 196–197
Products
benefit claims for, 58–59. See
also Unique Selling
Proposition (USP)
brand loyalty to, 57
knowledge of, 57–58
market survey on, 184–185
personality for, 161
promotable features of, 164
quality of, 149
reputation of, 71, 160
Product specification sheet, 200
Professional publications, 42, 179
Unique Selling Proposition (USP)
for, 70–71
Psychology, in advertising, 52–78
Public address announcements, in
retail stores, 158
Public relations
advertising and, 19
See also Institutional advertising
Public service advertising, 156
Punctuation, excessive, 81

Radio advertising
copywriter role in, 2
copywriting for, 131–137
as medium, 35–36
music in, 132–133, 134
one-person organization for, 17
sound effects in, 133, 135(fig.)
television audio replay for, 36
Radio spot
format of, 133–134
live, 136(fig.), 137
number of words in, 131
print back-up to, 35–36
recorded, 134, 135(fig.), 137
time selection for, 35
Reader inquiry service cards, 179
Reply cards, postage-paid, 122,
123(fig.)
Reprints, 177

Research
  for media selection, 26
  See also Copy research
Retail advertising
  campaigns, 156–159
    duration of, 156–157
    goals of, 157, 159
    image building in, 158–159
    principles of, 157
    tactics in, 157–158
  co-op material for, 175
  copywriter role in, 2
  copywriting for, 14–15
  media selection for, 28
  one-person organization for, 17
  research for, 183
  Unique Selling Proposition (USP)
    in, 66–67
Retail stores
  ad merchandising by, 179
  direct mail advertising for, 124–
    125
  merchandising in, 18
  national campaign tie-ins to, 167
  Point-of-purchase displays in,
    42–44
  traffic building devices for, 157,
    159
Reverse technique, 31
"Ride the showing," 45
Robinson-Patman Act, 173
Rough layout, 96–101
Run of the paper (ROP) position,
  29

Sales force, campaign presentation
  to, 170–171
Sales presentation, 170–171
Scripts
  for radio spots, 134–137
  for television commercials, 137
    camera movements in, 139–
      140
    camera positions in 138–139
    format of, 141–142
    sample of, 144(fig.)
    technical terms in, 140–141

SCW, Inc. (Stamps-Conhaim), 110
Sentences
  length of, 81
  number of, 83
Service campaigns, 152–153
Seventeen Magazine, 179
Shoot to the layout, 199
Signature, in print ad, 89, 96
Simplicity, as copywriting rule, 76–
  77
Slice-of-life format, in television
  commercials, 142
Slogans, 158, 160–161
Sound effects, in radio advertising,
  133, 135(fig.)
Space salesman, in newspaper
  advertising, 16
Split runs
  in mail order advertising, 126,
    128
  as research tool, 190
Standard Rate & Data, 29
Standard Rate & Data, for business
  publications, 42
Standard Rate & Data, for spot
  radio, 35
Starch, Daniel, 190–191
Storyboard, in television
  commercials, 137, 142, 143,
  145
Subhead, in print ad, 89, 96, 98,
  107

Target audience
  pre-testing of, 189
  selection of, 53–55
Target Response Statement. *See*
  Unique Selling Proposition
  (USP)
Television advertising
  audience attention in, 141
  commercial form in, 142–143
  commercial post-testing in, 191–
    192
  copywriter role in, 2
  copywriting for, 137–146

Television advertising (*Continued*)
  film *vs* tape in, 143, 146
  as medium, 36–37
  script directions in, 138–141
  script format in, 141–142,
    144(fig.)
  storyboard in, 137, 142, 143,
    145(fig.)
  technical terms in, 140–141
  time factor in, 65
  timing of, 36–37
Testing. *See* Post-testing; Pre-
  testing
Test markets, 192
Thomas Register, 51
Tie-in advertising
  for dealers, 173
  for retailers, 167
Time, special editions of, 38
Time factor
  in broadcast advertising, 130
  in magazine advertising, 118
  media selection and, 65
Trademark protection, 104(fig.)
Trade publications, 42, 179
  Unique Selling Proposition (USP)
    for, 67–70
Transit advertising, 49–50
Typesetting, tips on, 196–197
Typing requirements, for copy
  sheet, 92–94, 103

Unique Selling Proposition (USP),
  118, 142
  for advertising campaigns, 150,
    156, 161–162, 163–164
  audience motivation and, 71, 74–
    75
  company image and, 71
  industrial, 70
  national, 61–66
  product attributes in, 65–66
  professional, 70–71
  retail, 66–67
  trade, 67–70

Verb, tense of, 81
Visual sheet, 90, 92
  doodle layout in, 94–96
  rough layout in, 96–101

Whip shot, 140
Window displays, 157, 173
Words
  excessive, 81
  number of, 83
    in radio spots, 131
  syllables in, 85
Writings. *See* Copywriting, style
Writing Yardstick, 83–85

ZIP codes, as income indicator, 189
Zoom shot, 139